POWERED

BY WELLESLEY

(I)

Jin Lan McCann

ISBN-10: 0-9989899-9-1

ISBN-13: 978-0-9989899-9-0

AUTHORED BY JIN LAN MCCANN

EDITED BY NEWGRANGE PRESS

COVER DESIGNED BY: ALEXANDER VALCHEV

This memoir is dedicated to all the people who loved and nurtured me. Especially, my beloved parents who gave me life and unlimited love, my husband William D. McCann who gave me rebirth, joy of life and inspirations, my parents in law Doris K. Steckel and Steward Steckel who helped me to understand what means to be free, and always gave me unconditional love and support.

For Dan.

Jin Lan McCann

輝耀嵐

Foreword

On the beautiful campus of Wellesley College, a blue banner with white letters says, "Wellesley Women Are Growing Roots and Wings." On my coffee mug, it says, "Wellesley College - Where the Coffee is Strong, the Women Stronger." Yes, this school empowers women to change the world for the better.

I entered Wellesley College at age 42 to improve myself and see what I could do for the world. I have always wanted to make differences, from small to big. I even saved someone from the death penalty. I always wished I could contribute my passion, energy and talent for the societies which nurtured me and/or need me.

So, here I find myself at a prestigious women's school that gathers various kinds of the smartest people in the world, as though in a dream that I never could imagine. People here often ask me the same question: "What brought you to Wellesley?" The question always takes me back to my far away hometown Chongqing, and my childhood.

My hometown Chongqing is the largest and most populous city in China, although people in the West might not have heard about it at all. It's a mountain city, a gateway to Southwestern China, and the economic center of the upper Yangtze River. It has 32 million residents, a number increasing by 500,000 per year, and with a GDP growth of 20% plus annually. It is the 3rd largest center of automobile manufacturing and the largest motorcycle-producing region in the country. More than one hundred Fortune 500 companies have established a presence in the city. Sales of food, beverages, tobacco, alcohol, jewelry, office supplies, clothing and other textiles increased by 45% during 2009. It is reported as having beautiful women, a rising metropolis in its infancy, and there seems no way to stop it. The problem is that if its residents do not implement clean ways to develop, development will occur with all the pollution it entails.

For the past ten years, I had not seen a single star in the sky of Chongqing, let alone the blue sky and white clouds I used to see when I was little. I envisioned an even more terrible picture of Chongqing, more cancers, worse air...and decided to travel to the West to see what I could do to make a difference. As one might have sensed by now, I am an optimistic woman with dreams, and always have a positive attitude looking into the future.

As this is being written, the American people have rejected a Wellesley graduate who spent her life fighting for human rights as its first woman President. Instead, it has elected a swashbuckling man who does not speak softly in order to make people believe he carries a big stick. However, if the United States is strong enough to adopt and nurture a willowy Chinese woman and turn her into a force for change, it can survive anything - even a President who purportedly believes global warming is a hoax and we should hide behind his walls of trade and immigration. We shall see, shall we not? As I lead you through the fantastic story of my life and the modern Chinese history, you will conclude that the audacity of hope trumps any lesser emotion.

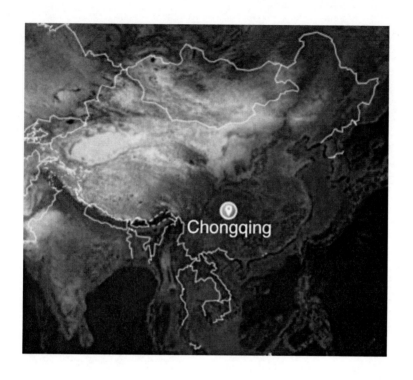

Map of the People's Republic of China

Pictures of Chongqing

Pictures of Chongqing

BOOK I

Contents

Splendid Morning Dew

I just translated my talented high school classmate's

new poem from Chinese into English:

Birth Place

Whenever I needed to fill in a birth place form,

I always sincerely inscribed:

'Chongqing Obstetrics and Gynecology Hospital'.

Every time, someone pointed out:

You only need to write down 'Chongqing,'

Every time, I stubbornly shook my head.

I knew, during those disastrous years,

to safeguard the same idol,

even family members would kill each other.

This city owned numerous weaponry manufactures,

working class members drove tanks into the streets,

set sail warships upon the Yangtze River,

targeted schools with canons . . . .

For one born in a Hospital,

life was guaranteed from the beginning.

How lucky this was,

but more people in my time

were given birth on narrow, humid

hard boards in the darkness,

in range of flying bullets,

in the domain of missile explosion coverage.

Their first cry could not break through

the cotton quilt insulated windows,

even some of them died before their first cry

could be deliver to earth.

- By Yu Yan, 2016[1]

Yu Yan and I both were born in February 1967, the beginning of the notorious Cultural Revolution, China's historic 'dark age'. This poem is a depiction of the crazy environment into which I was born. However, my other friend Buddha, who was a teenager at that time, told me what he *saw* was much worse than the poem *depicted*.

My Mom used to mention the armed fights during the beginning of the Cultural Revolution. She thought that Cultural Revolution was supposed to be a civilized debate about how people should run the country. Instead, the people who could not win the debate resorted to violent repression of each other, because Chairman Mao Ze Dong[2] said

---

[1] Please notice that this poem is very current. Why now? Because history doesn't necessarily repeat, but at least it rhymes. Both Yu Yan and I saw the pattern that China is on the reflection point of repeating history. Whether this society can avoid the tragedy happen again, it is many people's concern.

[2] Please know that to protect the Chinese friends I mention in this book, I have translated their first names into English and will not record last names. Chairman Mao Ze Dong will hereinafter be referred to as Mao. High officials and celebrities will be given their original full names in

---

"Power comes from guns," and the people treated what he said to be Gospel just as the westerners treat what is said in the Bible to be true.

Mom used to complain to me that sometimes she did not even have any food to eat for a whole day while hiding in the bomb shelter to avoid flying bullets and eye-less missiles. However, I, an infant, kept crying in her arms for milk. Now I feel sorry for her and wish I could have been a better infant.

The name of my eldest brother is History, given by my Mom's father, named Clean Life[3]. History is seven years my senior. He told me a story about the bomb shelter era.

Chinese order, which is the last name first, followed by the first. For teachers and clients, I will only give their last name without translation.

[3] Clean Life is my maternal Grandfather's name. Chinese people's names usually represent parents' expectation of their children. However, read through my stories: you will find that, sometimes, the character of particular individual is the opposite of their name.

One day, when all my family members were hiding in the bomb shelter under the building of the Yangtze Shipping Co., where my Father worked, my Grandfather became so hungry he had to make some food to eat. Thus, he desperately fled home with my brother History. Since he did not want to see the flying bullets outside the uncurtained window, he draped the window with a bed sheet. While he was standing on a stool so doing, a bullet broke through the glass window and lodged in the wall. My Grandfather was so shocked, he fell to the ground, cried out and pissed. History thought this most funny and laughed at my Grandfather.

My brother told this story to me when he was 37. I told him it was *not* funny because my Grandfather could have been killed by that bullet. How lucky for History that he was too young to realize fear.

In order to understand my childhood, one must understand what the Cultural Revolution is, how it happened, what its impacts are and why it is controversial.

So, what is The Cultural Revolution?

Some Westerners misunderstood the Cultural Revolution as a time when the Chinese government repressed its people. This can only be true if you call Orwellian governance a government, since everyone was spying on everyone else during that time. In fact, my parents told me, the bureaucratic machine was disabled by the Red Guards who were teenage students encouraged by party Chairman Mao, and they began to play the role of governance.

It was a violent movement initiated by Mao, in the name of democracy, to restore ideologically pure communism (Maoism) – as distinguished from the pragmatic socialism implemented by state Chairman Liu Shao Qi. Liu Shao Qi was Mao's internal political rival in the communist party. Mao, obviously, did not want to be China's

George Washington, a man who left power after his two terms as the first president of the United States.

The full name of the movement is **The Great Proletarian Cultural Revolution.** It also marked Mao's return of power from his failed practice of extreme communism, the Great Leap Forward, that caused serious famine. Since then, Maoism functioned like monotheistic religion during the dark age of Europe. Maoism was the only belief permissible if one wanted to survive.

In retrospect, the elements of the Cultural Revolution are: mind control, destruction of the rule of law and traditional culture, demonizing the West, disrespect for intellectuals, violation of basic human rights. These elements were not only factors in forming the constructs of my early childhood, they are still active today in governing the daily lives of Chinese people.

How Did The Cultural Revolution Happen?

When the Chinese Communist Party took power from the Qiang Kai Shek government[4] in 1949, Mao was both the chairman of the communist party and the state until 1959. In order to turn China into a modern industrialized country with surreal speed, Mao abandoned the communist party's promises of developing a democracy and allowing a portion of the economy to be private. In 1958, he started a Great Leap Forward movement that prohibited private businesses, even home kitchens. This movement caused the death from starvation of 36,000,000 human beings. In Xin Yang, Henan Province folks ate the dead bodies of their neighbors. A teenage girl killed her four years old brother and ate his body, according to Yang Ji Sheng, a former journalist from China's state news agency.

The manpower that should have been used on food production was misallocated to produce steel and weapons.

---

[4] Qiang Kai Shek's government escaped to Tai Wan towards the end of the Civil War in 1949.

Mao made people believe that the escaped Qiang Kai Shek government might retaliate against mainland China some-day, or foreign empires might invade China again. Almost all levels of government exaggerated local outputs of food while in fact there was not much food stored in the barns.

Due to Mao's failed practice of extreme communism during his two terms in office (1949-1959), the succeeding Chairman of the State, Liu Shao Qi, adopted a pragmatic strategy. He redistributed land and other resources to fami-lies. His polices improved the economy significantly in a couple of years. However, his economic success came with the price of social conflict.

Chinese history developed a custom that participants of revolutions should obtain government offices upon vic-tory, no matter their level of competence. There was a sig-nificant number of uneducated leaders in the government Mao's accession to power in 1949. So, the educated leaders wanted the uneducated leaders to retire. Besides, some of the redistribution of resources was not fairly done. An enormous group of people, mostly uneducated, believed that the new policies meant a switch towards a capitalist economy instead of a communist economy as the party promised. They complained about the arrogance of educated elites which had torn down peasant houses to build airports or other public facilities without proper negotiation with the property owners. They also complained about other corruptions, such as unfair distribution of resources and job opportunities among politically connected and unconnected families. Mao received massive complaints against the bureaucracy and heard that the peasants were kneeling in front of the cadres begging for justice.

Mao took the opportunity to criticize the new administration. He pointed out that the peasants were supposed to be the owners of the country and able to stand up to the authorities. Instead, they were kneeling before the authorities begging for justice. Thus, **the seeds of the Cultural Revolution were sewn**.

In May 1966, Mao accused the Liu Shao Qi government society of infiltrating the society with bourgeois elements. He started the Cultural Revolution to remove capitalist roots by a continuous class struggle, breaking traditions and challenging authorities. He initiated the revolution in the high school of Qing Hua University by sending his wife Jiang Qing to relay his order, and China's youth around the country formed Red Guard groups in response to Mao's appeal. Since then, they have behaved as the most loyal Maoists. They so behave today.

The government machine had been brainwashing the society with extreme communist ideology everyday for a decade under Mao's rule (1949-1959). To protect the party's image, Chairman Liu Shao Qi did not openly criticize Mao's wrong policies. The movement by the brainwashed Red Guards swiftly spread to all over the country including

---

the military, urban workers and the Communist Party leadership itself. Teenagers left their schools and jumped on trains to go to Beijing to visit Mao. Revolutionary slogans were everywhere on vehicles and buildings; many of them contained fallacies and perverted common sense. For example, one slogan was "Long Live the Proletariat Dictatorship." This slogan sounds as though the people would love to stay poor forever. Another slogan proclaimed, "We would rather have socialist grass instead of capitalist seedlings."

To get rid of the capitalist seedlings, the Red Guards purged all leaders who supported Chairman Liu Shao Qi and vice Chairman Deng Xiao Ping. Since Liu Shao Qi failed to communicate effectively with the student leaders and resorted to suppress the most radical elements of the movement, he was tortured to death by the Red Guards. Mao had to put vice Chairman Deng Xiao Ping in

----

jail to protect him from being killed by Mao's fanatic fol-
lowers.

The Cultural Revolution was conducted under the
name of democracy and supposed to be a civilized political
campaign. However, millions of people were violently repressed and abused across the country when the zealous
Red Guards tasted the power of majority. Basic human
rights were violated, public humiliation, arbitrary imprisonment, torture, sustained harassment, and seizure of private property, were not uncommon during the time. Tian
Han,[5] who wrote the revolutionary national anthem, was
condemned as an anti-revolutionary revisionist and died in
jail. Many people were unwillingly displaced from their
hometowns to rural regions, mostly, scholars and urban
highschool graduates. Historical relics and artworks were
destroyed, cultural and religious sites were ransacked, and

---

[5] He is in picture 4.

Picture 1. Expel the traitor, hidden traitor, scab Liu Shao Qi from the party forever

Picture 2. Thoroughly expose and criticize Liu Shao Qi's monstrous crime of treason

Picture 3. This cartoon denounces Liu Shao Qi's pro-free market

Picture 4. Anti-revolutionary revisionist Tian Han

----

family ethics were abandoned. It was into this chaos that I was born.

What are the impacts of The Cultural Revolution?

Normally, societies must achieve balance between competition and cooperation to develop efficiently. Competition may improve our individual strength while encouraging our greed, cooperation may integrate individual strength while testing our tolerance and persistence. To achieve fair competition and cooperation, societies must establish and maintain the rule of law while breaking old traditions. The Cultural Revolution accomplished the goals of breaking traditions and challenging authorities, but destroyed the rule of law and the ability to think rationally.

As much as I had been brainwashed by the government machine for the most of my life, I can only see one positive impact of the Cultural Revolution. That is, it boosted the confidence of some poor people as owners of the country when they broke traditions and challenged authorities. This is important, because, if you don't feel you are an owner of the country, then you might consider yourself a slave of the ruler. A slave can't produce as much GDP as a free man can. The Cultural Revolution made poor people feel proud that they became the owners of the country and no longer in the possessions of the powerful, for the first time in Chinese history.

However, at least three negative impacts can be blamed on the Cultural Revolution. When the Red Guards shut down government, churches, and raided households, they destroyed the tenuous foundation of the rule of law and proper manners of the society. Since then, Chinese people have developed the habit of violating or circumventing rules. If you see a pedestrian walking in the street of New York City against a red light, that pedestrian is likely a Chinese from mainland China.

In addition, the society's rational thinking deteriorated by slavish adherence to a political correctness demanded

----

by Maoists. When freedom of thought was monopolized by Maoism, that philosophy was defined as the only truth by the devoted Red Guards. One had to take a risk to tell the truth. To prove their loyalty to Mao, family members started to spy on each other and report each other for imagined political incorrectness. Many of the reported family members were sent to the countryside for reformation, thus family ethics were damaged.

After so many years of brainwashing by only one idea, many people in contemporary China can only see things as black or white. There is no middle ground, no concession or compromise. If all you read, including government newspapers and textbooks, convey what is reported to be the only truth, then there is no alternative. You are led to doubt the opposite opinion. There are no other concepts of truth. When speaking what you are taught as the only truth, you care little to hear what other opinions may be. The only truths are what were written and published by the communist party.

If you question certain ridiculous policies, people would tell you to always trust the party, because it is always right, bright and honorable. If you have a different opinion about certain policies, you may frequently hear people question you, "You think you are smarter than the government? Who do you think you are?" That is the kind of mind set that numerous Chinese people still have in the 21st century.

Why is The Cultural Revolution Controversial?

The Cultural Revolution is controversial because Chairman Mao brainwashed us to believe it was great revolution and we should continue it forever because class struggle was eternal and inevitable. This is contrary to what the post-Mao government told us. The post-Mao government characterized the Cultural Revolution as a mistake made by Mao since it caused ten years of social chaos and wasted a generation's optimum time for education and economic development. The government has never revealed to us what led Mao to make this mistake in his last ten years of life[6], and why there was such massive support for his mistake. The government just told us, "Let's not play at class struggle any more; we should focus on economic development." The topic of the Great Famine caused by Mao's Great Leap Forward movement is still taboo today.

Rumors abounded: some people believe Mao loved power too much and used innocent people's trust to attack his political rivals; others believe that it was a power struggle between the educated leaders and the uneducated leaders. Yet more believe there was a political struggle between

---

[6] One must remember, at the inception of the cultural revolution, Mao was 74 years of age. He was absolutely married to his own paradigms. Marriage to paradigms at that age is a decaying relationship. Its analogous, in a way, to why a 1950 Hudson Hornet is worth 20 or 30 times the price it sold for then. Some septuagenarian, married to his paradigms, is behind the wheel. From an intellectual point of view, Mao did not age gracefully.

the extreme communists and the moderate capitalist supporters who wanted a portion of the economy to be a free
market. The truth could comprise all these elements.

Advised by Mao, the Red Guards wanted to eradicate capitalist roots, because communist preachers told
them that capitalism may only help the 'haves' to exploit
the 'have nots.' The Red Guards viewed all small private
businesses, or land distribution to families, even home
raised chickens and pigs, as the seeds of capitalism. This is
certainly true, but the communist preachers' idea of capitalism as sin is wrong.

Even today, a lot of Chinese people refuse to believe that capitalism can be fairer for the working classes
than a planned economy. They would rather let all resources be controlled by authorities who might be ignorant
and/or corrupt. Many of them even naively believe government owned companies can operate on losing money
forever to achieve social stability.

When Marxism was taught in schools, we were told that monopoly was bad. Monopolies let the rich intentionally dump food into the trash and not feed the hungry people. We were told competition was bad. Competition forced so many small business owners to fail and jump off buildings. No one dared to point out that the essence of capitalism is fair competition: *fair at the starting point.* Capitalism may reduce exploitation of labor and producer surpluses. When capitalists expand, they hire more workers and eventually increase their wages while consumers enjoy cheaper prices of goods.

Mao never admitted or realized that constant high unemployment rates and shortages of almost everything were the results of nationalizing all resources. Instead, he blamed our shortage of everything on the Soviet Union since they required us to repay our loans. Or, he blamed our shortage of food on the weather.

One of the serious complaints about Mao was his insistence on never ending class struggle. It wrought not only social chaos, but also resulted in frequent shortages of food supply. Hunger was the most impressive image of my childhood.

In 1970, at the age of three, I remember one morning when my Mom slept very late, my Father had gone to work and my two elder brothers were at school. I ate a steam bun that my Father bought for me, gobbled it down fast. Not satisfied, I cruised around the table that held another steam bun. *That* one belonged to my Mom. I circled the table again and again, never taking my eyes off the bun.

I thought: 'the extra parts of the bun shaped by the steam container's bottom slats, should not *really* belong to the bun.' So, I tore those segments off and devoured them. Still not satisfied, I walked around my Mom's bed, and spoke to the air again and again: "One bun is so small, not enough."

Then, I walked back to the table and gazed at my Mom's steam bun and thought, again: "If the bun doesn't have the *skin*, it can still be called a bun." I tore the skin off and ate it. Still, not satisfied, I walked back to my Mom's bed, said to her: "You have such a big bun, I do not know how you can eat it all." Mom was surprised, but did not say a word. Years later, she questioned me, "How can a bun be too small for a small person and too big for a big person?"

Then, our neighbor, Uncle Song, the police chief, opened the door and asked me why my Mom did not get up and cook. He did not see our stove light up in our common kitchen. I told him that my Mom was still sleeping. He came in and put his hand on my Mom's head, then suddenly carried her away.

I became impatient waiting until my second brother Banyan came home from school. He is four years elder than I am: he was the naughty brother who caused trouble every day and liked beating me whenever he encountered

---

me. Banyan came in and immediately grabbed the bun on

the   table and devoured it.

I yelled at him, "That's Mom's bun!"

He answered, "Mom won't be home soon, because she is

sick and has to undergo an operation at the hospital."

I remember this vividly, because I never desired

steam buns as much as in that year. Also, later in that year,

we acquired an additional room on the third floor instead of

sharing one studio without a kitchen nor a toilet, as a family

of six. My Grandfather, parents, two elder brothers and my-

self shared this small space since my parents' marriage.

Such was the norm at that time in our society, and we were

not the worst off, because my Father was the party secre-

tary of a branch of the Yangtze Shipping Company, the

largest company in town, so he could afford to let my Mom

be a house wife.

I have never understood why my parents isolated

me in one room in my early years, with insufficient com-

----

munication or interaction. Since the age of three, I encoun-

tered my two elder brothers and my Grandfather only at

lunch and dinnertime.

Usually, we had no communication at all. Mom told

us not to talk while eating. After each meal, it was time for

me to go back to their bedroom which was on the third

floor. Except during sleeping time when my parents came

back, and meal times when my Mom brought me down to

the room which my Grandfather and two elder brothers

shared, I was alone in the room on the third floor.

My entertainment consisted of watching the Yang-

tze River through the window, or listening to the external

loud speakers repeatedly broadcasting quotes from Chair-

man Mao's red books, or playing songs in praise of him or

of the Cultural Revolution, all day long, each and everyday.

Naturally, I remember Mao's quotes much more

than my parents' quotes since my parents barely spoke.

Once, when I got bored because I had no toys at all and no

one to talk to, I saw a corner of my Mom's silk shirt sticking out from a locked leather suitcase. I pulled more fabric out of the case and found that it had pandas on it, so I embroidered all of them with thick blue cotton thread. When my Mom decided to wear that shirt, and found out what I had done to it, I got beaten with her tailor-made bamboo switch. My parents had the reputation of beating their children the hardest in our community, because, by their standards, they did not allow us to make any mistakes.

My Mom loved cleaning every corner of each room every day, and always made sure I was clean. She accomplished this by giving me a bath and washing my hair, each time made me feel as if I were boiling in hell. She always made sure that the water was hot enough for her, but too hot for me, as a baby. I still remember beating her face with my little fists while she was washing my hair. Of course, I also cried and screamed: "Beat you, this son of tortoise!

Beat you, this son of tortoise." (this is the equivalent of a well-known English curse)

My Mom washed me all over until I was thirteen. Later, I figured out each time she washed me consumed two hours. As I grew older, I used to joke with her after she finished washing me, "Now, it's ready to serve." She believed she was loving me by taking care of my every need. In any event, I just felt as though she was boiling me, but I did feel her deep love, because she spent so much time and energy on making sure I was always clean. Being clean was always a priority above all other things in my Mom's view.

Although I do not have any interesting memories other than painful ones about my childhood, I always believed that my Mom did everything for my benefit. Though I have never resented her, I always wanted to get away from her. I barely got a chance to leave the room. Whenever I was permitted to play outside for a while, I wanted to stay outside of her regime forever.

I remember one night when I was four or five, I was permitted to play outside of the room with neighbor kids all night long because the heat incinerated the room and we had no electric fan. I felt so happy that night, and did not want to return home at all, even though I knew my Mom was looking for me throughout the building. At midnight, I was hiding in the dark of the corridor while watching my Mom desperately searching and calling, "Third sister, third sister. . . . " I did not answer her even when she was very close to me, until I became so sleepy I could not keep my eye lids from closing. Only then, did I respond to her.

People might wonder whether I had a real name, since my Mom called me 'Third sister'. I did not know my name until age six and a half in the fall of 1973, on my first day of elementary school.

That morning, Mom pulled out a piece of paper, wrote three beautiful words on it, "Deng, Jin Lan," and taught me how to read it. She told me that this was my

----

name. Deng is my family name from my Father, Jin means Splendid and Lan means Morning Dew. She explained to me that she and my Father had always wanted a daughter after having two sons. So, when I arrived as the answer to their dreams, they did not let my Grandfather, the most educated man in the family, name me as he did my two older brothers. Mom loved the word 'Jin' because it was derived from a Chinese idiom, "Jin Shang Tian Hua," inscribed on each of their rice bowls received as wedding gifts. This idiom means "Adding a flower to an already splendid life." 'Lan' was my Father's idea, because Mom was The Flower in his eyes, so I was the morning dew on his flower.

I loved my name Splendid Morning Dew. However, it was too hard to write in Chinese, and until then, no one had ever taught me to read or write. Mom told me to remember my name and when the teacher called it out, I should answer.

Another thing I have never understood is why my Mom had not taken me to school on the first day. She let me follow the neighbor's kid to a school which I had never been. Did not she know that I barely left our building before, and did not have a clue where the roads led? Or how a school works? When she told me to follow the other kids to school, I did not imagine what might happen, just ran like a *wild horse* a name used by my Father to call me instead of my name Jin Lan. Perhaps, I wanted to escape from Mom no matter what.

Since I had never attended a kindergarten like the rest of the kids whose parents were both working, I thought that there was only one class in each school day. In fact, there were five, three in the morning and two in the afternoon. The first class was Chinese, taught by a very beautiful woman, teacher Gong, who spoke elegant mandarin and had beautiful hand writing. I loved every second of her lecture.

After the first class, I did not know there would be more and walked to the gate of the school. Another student saw me and told me I was going the wrong way. So, I followed her to another room in the second floor. It was a music classroom with a harmonica in the left corner beside the blackboard. The music teacher taught us a song about Sino-American friendship, I still remember one phrase: "I love Beijing-Washington, and Children of China and America laugh out loud, song of friendship throughout the world . . . ." This confused me, because in movies I had seen, people usually shout slogans such as, "Down with American Imperialism!" I held onto this confusion and enjoyed this class, but still did not know there was another class after this as well.

When the second class was over, I left the music classroom and walked out of the school gate. Once out of the school, I walked all the way to a crossroad, at which point I did not know which way I should go to get home.

Looking at the sky and the overhead wires for trolley buses hanging down, I recalled, before the Chinese class, one girl asked another whether she knew how to get home. The girl said, "Yes, my mom told me that I would never go wrong if I follow the overhead wires, because one way leads to her office, and the other way to home."

Since I knew her mom worked for the same company where my Father worked, and my home was on the opposite side of the street, aha! I would just follow the overhead wires too. I trailed a trolley bus for about twenty minutes, along a street with interesting shops and came to another cross road. Somehow, there was nothing which looked familiar, so I turned around and followed another trolley bus to home.

I was so excited after my first day of school, I did not know I had missed a mathematics class. When my neighbor came home, she told me I was absent from my mathematics class. I felt so embarrassed, but my Mom did

----

not notice this. I asked her why the American Empire that we were trying to beat down suddenly had became our friend. Mom took a piece of an old newspaper that had a picture of Dr. Henry Kissinger shaking hands with Chairman Mao on it and said, "Since Dr. Kissinger visited Chairman Mao, we are no longer enemies." She said it was good for China to have America as our friend instead of as our enemy, but she did not say why.

I maintained this confusion for more than 30 years, until one day when I told a high school classmate that I saw Dr. Kissinger playing in a magic show on the stage of the Bohemian Grove in California. My classmate said he always liked Dr. Kissinger. We grew up knowing his name and he changed our lives for the better. Later, I realized that Dr. Kissinger's visit to China not only meant more freedom and prosperity for China but also meant improvement of world peace. He ended the cold war and tactfully steered

China, this giant boat, toward the correct direction of civili-

zation.

The same afternoon, I went back to school and a

senior student read us a story of Chairman Mao. Then we

were told that we would have a big conference criticizing

Lin and Kong the next day. Lin had been the vice Chairman

of the country before his airplane crashed two years before.

Kong, pinyin for Confucius, had been dead for almost 2,

500 years. I was told we had to prepare for this critique and

each one of us would be required to get on the stage and

speak out.

Of course, I could not write a speech since I only

knew three words, "Mao Zhu Xi" which means Chairman

Mao, because it was inscribed everywhere. I still could not

write my own name! The next day, I brought with me a

written speech my eldest brother History wrote for me.

When my turn came, I bravely stepped onto the

stage, pretended that I could read as well as that senior stu-

---

dent familiar with Mao's story. Of course, I could pretend for less than one minute, and my teacher took away my paper and read from it, criticizing Lin, who allegedly betrayed Mao, and then, Confucius, the great thinker, educator and philosopher that Chinese people had worshiped for over 2000 years.

Basically, the speech repeated what Mao said: "We should challenge the authorities, because it was their dogmas which retarded the development of our Chinese people. Confucianism told us to obey and not to challenge authority, because he only spoke for the ruling class, not the working class." I only realized this was not true until 30 years later. The Cultural Revolution went on for ten years but never resulted in a democratic solution for social development. Mao never gave his opposition the chance to compromise, just like the communist party never gave Qiang Kai Shek's government a chance to compromise. Mao allowed the Red Guards to torture his longtime revolutionary fellow fighter,

----

Chairman Liu Shao Qi, to death. Instead of letting the government listen to their voices, the Red Guards shut them up and sent so many of the educated elites and whoever else disagreed with them to live with pigs and cows in the countryside.

Class Struggle games went on every day and everywhere for a decade. Mao instructed his people to never stop. I think, if Dr. Kissinger did not sneak into China and talk to Mao in 1972, God himself only knows whether the great famine might have happened again, since there was no one powerful and skillful enough to influence a change in China's political direction.

So, my education started late, but began at a pretty high level. That a six years old kid was required to criticize

Pictures of Chairman Mao Meeting Dr. Kissinger

and President Nixon

----

an almost 2,500 years old philosophy was a big joke to my Grandfather[7]. When my naughty brother Banyan remarked that my Grandfather looked like a bad guy because he had a beard like Confucius from the cartoon pictures, my Grandfather responded that it would be *great* if he could be Confucius! Banyan and I both thought my Grandfather was anti-revolutionary, a state of mind considered extremely bad at that time. He could have been put in jail if he had said the same thing to someone outside of the family.

After I had learned how to count, I realized the slogan "Chairman Mao Lives for Ten Thousand Years" represented an impossibility. I asked another girl how that could be possible. She swiftly covered my mouth with her hand and told me to shut up. Otherwise, I might be taken to jail or bring trouble to my parents. I could not understand the logic of asking an honest question as considered a criminal

---

[7] My Grandfather's picture is on the following page.

My Grandfather Clean Life

act. That was the first time I came to know everyone was frightened by *something*, although I did not know what it was. Also, several of my father's colleagues, who I usually encountered every day, hung themselves in the Sailor's Club. No one told us why. I still remember one of them was a very handsome middle-aged man, whom we referred to as Uncle Ke. He always greeted me with a big smile on his face. Before he dangled from the rafters, that is.

My Mom told me people had to recite a quote from Mao's Red Book or a praise of Mao before starting any conversation. So, instead of greeting people with "Have you eaten?" people had to say, "*Revolution is not a tea party,* have you eaten[8]?" Or, when a man needs to buy a steam bun, he had to say things like, "*Don't ever forget class struggle,* I want a steam bun." My Mom told me one day she called my Father on the phone to discuss Banyan's

---

[8] "Have you eaten?" means "how are you?" in Chinese custom.

health. My Father responded to her "'Class struggle is like the rim of a fishing net, once the rope is pulled out, all its mesh open,' how are you doing?" If one failed to quote from the Red Book, he or she could be endangered.

This is how intensively brainwashed our society was and the effects still vibrate the subconscious. When keywords are injected into the brain repetitively, they make people believe that the *injected* ideas are their *own* thinking or belief. This technique was not an invention of Mao: it was used in the Nazi propaganda to "Make Germany Great Again!"

In school, we were taught to love Chairman Mao and the communist party, and swore to do so. This was based on the teaching that the communist party, led by Mao, liberated poor Chinese from the repression of the Three Mountains: imperialism, feudalism and bureaucracy in collusion with capitalism. I enjoyed those revolutionary stories and their heroes.

I guess, all the kids might had secretly fallen in love with Mao and the party heroes, *except* my second brother Banyan. When we played games, everyone wanted the role of a communist party leader or a revolutionary solder. Banyan always wanted to be a high official of the Kuomintang government[9] who were characterized as evil guys at that time. We were told that the Qiang Kai Shek government was incredibly corrupt and repressive to its own people, since it had killed numerous communists. Banyan put cardboard in his cap to mimic military figures he had seen from the movies, and drew a Kuomintang army insignia on the front of his cap. Not only that, he even drew an array of bullets on the belt of his schoolbag. Also, there was a Kuomintang insignia on his schoolbag. My parents could not understand why he always wanted to play the evil guy, while everyone else wanted to be a communist hero.

---

[9] Kuomintang means Chinese Nationalist Party of the Republic of China, led by Qiang Kai Shek then.

No matter what my parents did, they could not change Banyan's preference to mimic ruthless Kuomintang high officials that he saw in the movies. My parents always worried that Banyan could continuously bring us trouble. That, he most certainly did.

At the start of the second semester of my first grade, my Grandfather died. I did not cry, although I missed him. Not because I did not love him, but because I had not built a strong enough emotional connection with him since we did not have much interaction. I always saw my Mom yelling at him and did not understand why. My Mom cried all day and every day for over a month after his death. I could not understand why she fought with my Grandfather almost every single day when he was alive, and then cried so hard at his loss. She did not explain the reason until 20 years later.

I hungered so much for knowledge, and received perfect grades each semester for two years, but my parents believed this was as it should be and never complimented me. They fed and clothed me well, and in exchange, I had to study well. If I got an imperfect score on a test like Banyan invariably did, my ass would get beaten like his, with my Mom's tailor-made bamboo switch.

My Father was not a sailor like most of the other parents in my class. My teachers favored students with sailor parents, because sailors could buy commodities cheaper from the countryside for them. For two years, I never had a teacher recommend me as a candidate for captain of the Young Pioneer Team, or any other leadership position. I was the best student and ambitious to play a more significant role. In fact, I was a natural leader in our adolescent community. About a dozen kids followed me whenever I was home. I was very disappointed with a school which treated me as invisible.

When our third year began, one night, I heard my parents chatting about my Father's colleague whose wife

----

was the Principal of another school. I decided to transfer to that school without consulting them. The next day, when I went to school, I confronted my Principal and asked for my transfer paper. He thought it was my parents' decision and gave me the paper. So, I brought it to my parents who were shocked, because we had never discussed it. However, I just told them I made the decision to transfer because I believed I would do even better in another school. I did not tell them why. That evening, my Father brought me to his colleague's home. His wife welcomed me right away, and I went to her school the next day.

My decision was correct. I was introduced to the class by the Principal. Before they elected a new captain of the Young Pioneer Team, I was recommended as a candidate by the instructor in charge of our class. Since she introduced me as a perfect student, although no one knew me then, all the students voted "yes" for me. School then became much more fun than before, with new activities. I fi-

----

nally had the life I wanted and even made a friend with the girl who shared the same desk with me. Cultural Flood was he name, she lived nearby, so I spent a lot of time at her home because her parents allowed much more freedom than my parents did.

Later that year, Banyan secretly begged me to help him transfer to my school, because he was in trouble. Banyan's school shared the same building with the hospital that belonged to the shipping company. One night, he collected the spittoons from all over the hospital, and placed them on the stairway of the school before the students came to evening class. He then turned off the main power switch of the building when he saw some girl students approaching the staircase. The girls were scared to death when they crashed into the spittoons, and thought they were in the presence of ghosts, because the mortuary was near by. So, they screamed like bloody murder. This caused complaints not only from the students, but from the hospital as well, be-cause it could not run without power.

This was not Banyan's first mistake. He also broke the school's electricity meter with a basketball and hit sev-eral teachers including the vice principal of his school. He knew he was going to be kicked out of the school, and thus begged me for help, because he learned how I accom-plished my transfer.

I took him to see my new Principal, and she as-sumed Banyan was as a good student as I was, and wel-comed him. Soon thereafter, the principal of his old school called my Father to have a chat and told him that Banyan had not attended school for a week. When my Father came home, he tied Banyan to his bed and beat him badly with his leather belt.

Banyan was used to be beaten since the age of four. He always managed to do something shocking. He even buried alive a chicken belonging to our neighbor, the police

----

chief. He was only eight. My Mom had to apologize to our neighbor and bought a new chicken as compensation. Of course, Mom also punished Banyan by not letting him have dinner. Banyan resented such punishment, and every time when he was told he could not have dinner, he dropped a piece of coal in whatever my Mom was cooking. Coal did not go well with congee. So, he got beaten almost every weekend when my Father was home and did not have to work.

In the beginning of the forth grade, Chairman Mao died. I thought the sky was going to fall since I believed he was the only one holding it up for the Chinese people. Though it rained everyday for a long time, the sky did not fall. Many people cried and made paper flower rings for Mao each day. Such activities went on and on for months, and I developed very good handiwork skills. As the captain of the Young Pioneer Team, I did not need to attend class and guarded Chairman Mao's mourning hall with a red-

---

tasseled spear, for one week. Every morning, students and faculties came to the mourning hall to bow to Mao's picture. They looked truly sad and some of them cried. I felt guilty that I was not sad enough to cry.

That year, the school taught us to sing a song:

"The Party, the government, the army, the citizens, the students, east, west, south, north and the middle...the Party leads everything. . . .the always great, honored and correct Party united all the people together . . . . lead us forward."

None of us doubted the logic about how a party composed of human beings can be always correct, since we were brainwashed to always trust the party and treat it as our mother. Real life mothers only gave us our bodies, but the light from the party illuminates our souls. All revolutionary movies repeat the same thing, "Always trust the party, no matter what situation you are in." Usually, this was enunci-

---

ated when someone was wronged or could not understand a certain policy of the party.

Many years later, after my Wellesley education, I found that Mao's communist construction was outrageously optimistic. He only focused on cooperation without providing solutions for problems such as: free loaders, asymmetric information, discouraged creativity, curbed entrepreneurial spirit, and political dissent. Probably, there was no solution to these problems in a planned economy without the rule of law.

His extreme communist economic model had more serious problems than he could imagine. It lacked the guidance of the invisible hand, the market price, to gauge production and efficiently allocate resources. Besides, it had the drawback of diseconomies of scale which means a business may lose efficiency due to oversizing. When everything was nationalized, the country became a gigantic business.

To control the society, the government confined generations of peasants to the land. They could not work and live in the cities, because they did not have the ration tickets only issued for urban people to buy food and other commodities. In cities, the prices of food were set by the government to guarantee that every family could afford to eat. While we as urban people enjoyed relatively sufficient food, we did not know that the peasants who produced the food were not guaranteed their fair share to prevent huger.

However, I still think that a successful communist society can be achieved in small scale communities that compete in a genuine free market with an effective rule of law. For example, any one of the top American universities that has a need-blinded policy for tuition and expenses can be viewed as a communist community, because it meets the requirement of "everybody tries his or her best and everybody receives what he or she needs." Therefore, the Harvard community succeeds as a team, just as in a big family where everyone tries his or her best and everyone receives whatever he or she needs. By the way, such communist communities must be achieved by the free will of community members instead of imposition.

After Mao died in 1976, Deng Xiao Ping and his supporters swiftly took power from Mao's appointed successors and told us that Cultural Revolution was a mistake made by Mao, and it was over. The educated elites gradually returned to their posts and they viewed Mao as a power addict instead of the great leader as described by the government machine before. Such opinions were underscored in the books written by educated Chinese who immigrated to the West in the 80's, but, we were told the opposite when in school. I never doubted that the school might tell us lies and did not know that the teachers' freedom of knowing and telling truth was limited.

My Mom always interpreted government announced news contrary to what she was being told, and

---

thus was not happy with the school's brainwashing of her kids. She thought I was stupid to believe in everything the school taught. On the other hand, she forbade me to tell the truth if it was contrary to the government voice, because it could be dangerous for me and the family. I had been confused by my Mom and the government machine's teaching.

For a long time, I believed that my Mom was the type of cynical person the government criticized, because she seemed to disagree with all the other people. Now I feel so sorry that I trusted my own Mom much less than I trusted the party, which controls the government and almost everything in the country. We were told to always trust the party and never doubt it, just like the western people trust God.

The new government gradually returned some freedom to its people. The political atmosphere was less intense than Mao's time, but the government still repressed political dissidents. Using the guise of social stability, dissidents are still not allowed to tell the truth publicly, and face the risk of being arrested.

Contrary to the conduct of the naughty Banyan, History was a perfect big brother who always did everything correctly, and protected me from Banyan's abuse whenever he could. I do not know whether he ever feared my parents, because he had never been punished for anything. Banyan had always feared my Father and I had always feared my Mom, because it was my Father's job to beat Banyan, and my Mom's job to beat me.

Since I was so afraid of my Mom, I did not tell her that once I almost drowned in the Yangtze River while trying to save my classmate. In the summer of 1981, I was admitted to Bashu high school. This an elite high school in Sichuan province, the same school which our future First Lady Mrs. Hu Jin Tao attended. Admission to this school was quite an honor at that time. However, my parents believed that this was only as it should be, so I re-

----

ceived no reward other than a promise that my Mom would

not beat me anymore when the new semester started.

Another important occurrence that summer was the

overflowing of the Yangtze River. Its water reached the

street, and many families lost their homes and loved ones in

the flood. When my old friend Cultural Flood heard that we

would no longer attend the same school, she invited me to

watch the flood together.

So, we walked along the river hand in hand in the

flood water, but she fell off a submerged cliff into deep wa-

ter. No one tried to save her, although thousands of people

walked by. I knew I could not leave her alone, and if she

had to die, then I had to go with her, because she was my

best friend and we had set out together. Neither of us could

swim, and we struggled for about 20 minutes to reach the

shore. It felt like forever.

Luckily, I grabbed a hole in a big stone and I still

had her hand in mine, so I dragged her close to the shore

and we climbed to safety with exhausted bodies. After we got out of the water, I did not dare walk home directly, because I was afraid that Mom would beat me or yell at me on account of my wet and dirty clothes. Until then, Mom *still* washed me and my clothes.

I went to my Father's office building, rinsed myself in the toilet, and went home in the dark. Mom did not notice me, because by the fifth grade (1978), we had moved to a new home. It had two bedrooms, a living room with our own kitchen and shared a toilet with our neighbor, all still by the Yangtze River. So, I had my own bedroom for the first time in my life when I was ten. Before that, I slept in my parents' big bed.

When Fall semester began, I became a boarder. I had lots of fun being away from my strict parents, and enjoyed ultimate freedom by not focusing on studies, relying on Mom's new policy of no more punishment for imperfect grades. In the first month, a boy from another class called

Building China wrote me a love letter and invited a dozen students to picnic in the zoo during National Holidays. I went to the picnic, but did not want to date him, because dating was not allowed in high school and I knew nothing about him. So, I wrote him back telling him that both of us should focus on studies and he could be my brother. He accepted this suggestion and we exchanged several letters in the name of sister-brotherhood.

Besides science courses, I enjoyed English the most. One of our three English teachers was teacher Chen, almost 70 years old. He spoke in a British accent and taught us several English songs. One of them was the English version of *La Marseillaise,* a revolutionary song of freedom. 20 year later, when I unconsciously sang this song in front of my American husband Bill, he asked me where I learned it. I told him that I was taught this song in high school, then he said it was incredible that my high school could teach us an anti-communism song. The truth was, none of us knew this was an anti-communism song!

Then I recalled, one time, teacher Chen came into our classroom with a winter fur hat, a woolen scarf, a long fur coat, a short and thick cotton coat, a woolen sweater. . . .many layers of clothes. After he warmed up, he gradually took off his hat, scarf, long coat. . . .and piled them on the lecture desk. The boy sitting in front of him thought it was funny and said, "Come on, take them all off," then we all laughed out loud. When this happened, our class advisor, teacher Zhou, was monitoring our class through the window. He got angry and broke into the classroom, criticized us not cherishing such a wonderful English teacher that the school had tried so hard rehabilitate after his miss-treatment in jail.

We were told that teacher Chen was educated at Oxford. He came home from the UK to build his motherland. However, he did not know telling the truth was dangerous. He criticized Mao's policies when he was encouraged to do so, then he was jailed until my school desperately wanted good English teachers. While he was in jail, he translated all of Mao's red books. When I heard this, I thought he must have loved Chairman Mao so much to translate his books. Today, I realized that his real intention might be to let the world know what was in this tyrant's mind.

I felt so sorry that we did not cherish his efforts toward our education and were disrespectful to him. We were too ignorant to understand what he went through and did not much change our behavior. We still made noises while he was lecturing us. I think, we were just too numb to the other people's suffering and could not imagine what freedom means to a decent man. We were not only disrespectful to teacher Chen, we were the same to several other eminent teachers who had similar experiences as teacher Chen.

The result of having too much fun was that my grades dropped after two years. My class advisor, teacher Zhou, visited my parents at our new home by the Jialin River, a major branch of the Yangtze River. We moved to this home in Jan 1982. It had two bigger bedrooms, two patios, a natural gas pipeline supply, and a kitchen and a toilet. We never had our own toilet before, always shared with neighbors. By this time, my brothers had gone to college and moved out. When teacher Zhou found out that I had a big bedroom at my parents' home yet was crowded in with nineteen other students in one dorm, he asked my parents to take me home. Thereafter, I had to take early morning buses to go to school with no more lazy morning sleep.

Although I was still angry with teacher Zhou for this reason, I had lots of fun from commuting. I am grateful for his seeing great potential in me, something I could not envision by myself. He was indeed a loving and dedicated teacher.

Our new home was still on the tip of the peninsula formed by the Yangtze and Jialin Rivers. I had to rise every morning at 6:30 am, and walk down the street to take a bus since the school started at 7:15 am. The most impressive thing to me was the crowds. There were always endless lines of people who had to catch the buses during rush hour. To be able to get to school on time, I learned how to squeeze myself into an already very crowded bus. I used to bet with the School Flower[10] that I could catch any bus I wanted, because I did not care how I looked. She had to whip herself into perfect shape all the time, so she would rather miss a bus or be late for class than imperfect.

However, sometimes, I did regret that I squeezed myself into a super crowded bus, because I could not even give my small nose enough space to breath. One day, I boarded a bus as the last passenger and the weight of the

---

[10] School Flower was the most beautiful and popular girl in our school and my new friend in the class.

door closing squeezed me in. I found my hair in a crazy mess, my hands gripped the door like a lizard on a wall, and my nose was also squashed out of shape against the door. I could not breathe, and even if I could, I would only inhale a lot of CO_2 expelled by my fellow passengers. This was extremely uncomfortable during the summer heat, because some people were smelly. Other times, men pushed against girls like me in obscene ways.

One morning, I saw a very good-looking boy, ten years or younger, fall from a moving bus, the back wheel of which ran over one of his legs. I was surprised that the young boy did not cry, but stared at his leg and the huge hole that had opened in it. Two adults carried him away to the hospital. I remember the skin of his leg opening like a window in a wall. I could see the red flesh and blood vessels in his leg. This image has stayed with me forever, and I always wonder why his parents let him take buses alone to school when he was so young.

At times other than rush hour, I used to take a bus and travel all over the city for entertainment with the School Flower. It was just so much fun watching people walk around the city; this gave me a chance to learn the names of the streets. I had and still have a problem with directions. Every time I was separated from my Mom's hand when I was little, I had to be taken home by a cop, who found me in the street. Without taking so many buses, there was no way I would ever learn the streets of the city.

Because of my inability to adapt to the changes of my life, such as having to get up early every morning, I resented instructor Zhou and made a stupid mistake I shall regret forever. I gave him a bad nickname and wrote it in big letters on the blackboard. He was very offended and angry when he saw it. He invited my Mom to the school to have a chat.

During my first two years, my Mom had only gone to the school once to bring me a quilt for the approaching cold weather. When I told my Mom she had to meet instructor Zhou, she could not believe it, because she believed only naughty boy students precipitated parent meetings. She felt ashamed and refused to go. I told her if she would not go, then I wouldn't be admitted to class. So, she had to go, and she apologized to instructor Zhou for me. Later, I felt deeply sorry for what I had done to instructor Zhou, so I went to see him at his home several times after graduating from Bashu High School.

Although I did not pay much attention to my studies, my grades were not awfully bad due to my solid foundation. However, my confidence was seriously damaged for years by my scores from the college entrance test in 1984. The Chinese educational system gives only one chance each year for college entrance test. If you blow it, you must wait for another year.

When I encountered a math problem I could not solve, I was not prepared to abandon that problem and continue with the rest of the test. Therefore, I screwed up the whole test. I was so upset because I knew I could not get into any school I wanted with *that* grade. So, I was not in the mood to take the rest of the tests. My Mom observed me avoiding the rest of the tests, took out her tailor-made bamboo switch that had not been used for years, and beat me. Thereafter, I went, but was in no mood to do my best.

The result was not a surprise to me and I begged my Mom to give me another chance, and promised I would go to the best college in China if she me another chance. She rejected this idea, because the elite high school I had attended required one extra year of education than ordinary high schools. She thought she had already fed me for one more year than the other kids, and I should, therefore, be on my own.

I felt I was a failure and had no desire to face my classmates again. The problem eventually resolved at our 20th anniversary reunion in 2004. Once we got together again, we no longer wanted to be apart. Even today, we talk

on Wechat on daily basis, just like a big family. In fact, I

talk to them and have dinners with them more often than

with my own family members. Later, after I got married, I

took my husband to meet them, he was very impressed that

there were 60 of them at the welcoming party and he won-

dered how we could keep such a tight friendship for so long.

Me & the School Flower Ya Hong

My Mom

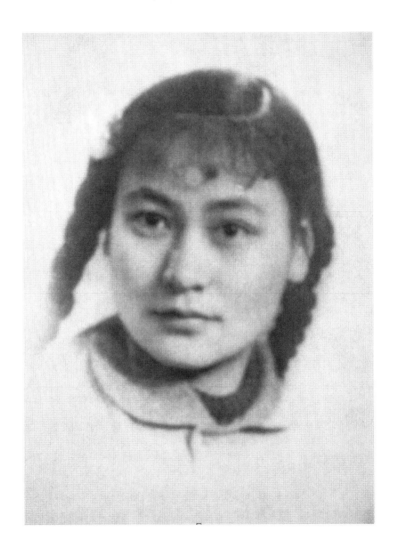

My Mom's name is Rich and Kind. Although she has never been rich materially, she has a rich spirit. She is always kind to the unfortunate.

I had very little communication with either of my parents when I was young. I did not understand why until the political atmosphere became much more relaxed. I used to tell my Mom that if my maternal Grandfather, was still alive I would spoil him with lots of love unlike how she treated him before he died. This sounded like blame to my Mom, and she always reacted to me: "You don't know anything, you have no right to say so." My Mom is not a person you can force to reveal what she does not want to tell. So, I lived with this puzzle until I became mature enough, at least in my Mom's eyes, to know.

My Mom is very reserved. I am different with her. I say what I mean and mean what I say. This bothers her a lot, because she thought that some day, my bold mouth might cause trouble, because in an environment that has no freedom of speech, wagging tongues can strangle a person when the Sky[11] changes. During her life, the political skies over China have changed multiple times.

I worked in government jobs since 1984, then quit my last government job in 1992 and became a successful business woman working for a Hong Kong commercial kitchen equipment company. In 1994 when I was 27, I bought a big condominium in a thirty-five floors high rise in the center of the richest city in China, Shenzhen, Hong Kong's neighbor city. I would fly my parents to Shenzhen every year to spend time with me. During my first year in the new condo, one day I criticized the government for doing something inefficient and stupid. My Mom fearfully told me to shut up.

---

[11] The Sky is my Mom's metaphor for political atmosphere, because in ancient China, the emperor was called "the son of the sky" or "the son of the heaven." Most Chinese people consider politics is only the business of the government, it has nothing to do with citizens.

I told her: "There's nothing to be afraid of, China is open to the world and it will never close again because once the majority of its people have tasted freedom, they will never go back."

She couldn't believe me and asked me with doubt in her voice: "Are you sure?"

As naive as I still was, to assure her, I explained: "The Chinese people supported the communist revolution because they had a bad life. 80% of the population were uneducated and illiterate before 1949, and they had never known what a normal life could be. Now people are educated and enjoying some freedom, they will only want more rather than less of what is precious to them." My communist education had provided us a poem:

> 'Life is precious,
>
> love worth more,
>
> for the sake of freedom,
>
> both can be abandoned.

- Petogfi Sandor "'"

My beautiful middle-aged Mom blinked her big shining eyes, and mysteriously asked: "Do you want to know why I always fought with your Grandfather when you were little?"

"Why? I thought you just had a bad temper and got angry easily."

"You do not know about a lot of things. I did not tell you because I was afraid that you would say something to the others who would cause trouble for our family. You are so innocent and everybody is a good and beautiful person in your eyes."

"Everyone is so nice to me though."

"Not really. They just pretended to be nice to you, because your Father was a respected executive in that company."

She was referring to our neighbors and our old colleagues in the shipping company. My parents always lived

----

in compounds with neighbors who worked in the same shipping company, because that was the norm in the old communist system. Housing was provided by the company for which one worked. Now, government owned companies no longer provide housing. Instead, people have free choice to buy wherever they like.

"I don't understand," I responded.

"Do you remember our old neighbor, Aunt Xing?"

"Yes, what?"

"Aunt Xing once told me that she was given a mission to spy on us by the police."

"She had been your best friend!"

"Yes, that's why she later told me the truth. She was told to make friends with me and get information to report to the police."

"Well, she did not have much to report."

"That is why I shut my mouth, because we *did* have something to hide."

"Weird, what could that be?"

"Your Grandfather. He did not behave like an ordinary clerk. He had a rich man's looks and style, so people suspected him."

"I thought he was just a bank clerk."

"It was not that simple! And we had relatives in Taiwan and the U.S. Do you remember when you were in high school, my niece Yong Lian visited us?"

"Yes, *that* was weird too, because I had never known you had such a relative until her visit. I thought we had no relatives except Wang Yu Li and her mother, who live in down town Chongqing!"

"Wang Yu Li is from my grandmother's side. Yong Lian is from my grandfather's side, and she has a younger sister called Yong Xia. The three of us used to play together when we were little. Then, when the Chiang Kai Shek government failed and fled to Tai Wan, both her parents and elder brothers got on the plane and left her and Yong Xia

----

with their wet nurse. Then the wet nurse took them to the countryside where she came from, and raised them."

"So, we have relatives in Tai Wan?"

"Yes, lots of them. Some of them immigrated to the U.S. in the 70's. They were well educated people, could have been successful anywhere. Yong Lian visited us, because her mom sent her a letter through a friend in Hong Kong, and she was trying to find a way to come to mainland China."

"So, *this* was why you were so angry with Grandpa? I still do not understand."

"It is much more than that."

So, my Mom told me about her unusual childhood. She was born in 1938, the year of the Tiger, and the second year of the 8 year long anti-Japanese War. She remembered the dark gray bombers flying over head almost everyday when she was little, because Chongqing was the temporary capital of the Chiang Kai Shek government.

During those times, people didn't know whether they would be killed by bombs that day or the next, so the rich just wined and dined, attended ballroom dances, gambled and smoked opium. My Mom's beautiful mother married my Grandfather Clean Life who was from a good family, well educated, and very handsome. Their marriage was almost perfect, and their first child was my Mom's elder brother, Bull. My Mom followed thereafter.

When she was very little, her mom contracted *menolipsis*, a kind of sickness that ended menstruation prematurely. She died when my Mom was just 2 years old. My Grandfather was very depressed because he believed it was his fault since he didn't take good care of my Grandmother due to his spoiled, self-centered, lifestyle. One relative told us my Grandfather had two maids caring for him since he learned to walk, one to play with him, the other carrying an extra set of clothes just in case.

Later, my Mom's elder brother Bull[12] also died due to some strange undiagnosed illness. Then, my Grandfather betrayed his name, Clean Life, by becoming addicted to opium. So, this superstitious family presumed it was my Mom's fault, because she was born in a Tiger year. They thought her overly strong life force might threaten all the weaker members of the family. Since then, my Mom was informally given to a relative's family and only allowed to call her own father "great uncle" instead of "papa" like ordinary kids do. She also had to address all her real family members as if they were just acquaintances.

When my Mom revealed this, it reminded me that when my Grandfather died, the neighbors who came to comfort her asked me why my Mom called her own Father "great uncle" instead of "papa." I did not know the answer, so did not give one. But, the recollection of her calling:

---

[12] Bull as in the bovine, not bull as in excrement.

"Great uncle! Great uncle! Wake up, it's your lunch time. You like Dan Dan noodles, here you are!" was so vivid. On this occasion, after she failed to rouse my Grandfather, she asked me to wake him up. I tried many times, but without success. I did not know he was already dead and went to school.

When I returned in the afternoon, a neighbor told me that my Grandfather died - and that my Mom was hysterical. I could not believe it. I thought he had woken up and eaten his noodles. I just could not believe how someone could look fine the day before, and then fall asleep and never wake up.

In fact, my Mom was excluded from her family since the age of two. After that, she barely saw her father and was told that he had gone to work for her real great uncle in Tian Jin, who was her father's eldest brother and a powerful man in the Chiang Kai Shek government. So, she either stayed at relatives' homes or stayed home alone like

----

an orphan. The rich relatives had numerous kids and grand-kids, wet nurses and maids. Their parents were so busy working, dancing, playing ma jiang, wining and dining that they did not have time for their own kids. I could only imagine how little attention my Mom received. She told me that no one noticed she was old enough to go to school, so she did not get an education until the communist seized power and required all citizens to learn to read.

My Mom told me that her father disappeared during the anti-Japanese War and Civil War time. Then he showed up when she was already working for an Army Hospital. This was in 1955 when she was 17. My Grandfather showed up at my Mom's workplace and asked about her life. She told him she had a handsome boyfriend who was a doctor at the hospital.

However, my Grandfather told her this was not a good choice because this man had too much education and would not treasure her as she deserved. Then he introduced

----

my Father to her and told her that my Father was working for the biggest company in Chongqing and a party official. This means a 'good protection' to people like my Grandfather who came from a former rich but now threatened family.

My Mom did not agree because she was in love with the doctor. My Grandfather pushed her to marry my Father because the political situation was growing serious. My Mom saw some of her classmates' fathers or relatives shot on the stage in public because they were capitalists. She was so scared and married my Father whom she did not love at all. They had nothing in common. My Mom grew up in a big city, whereas my Father's parents were fallen landlords. He grew up in the countryside of Hunan province. She cried immediately after their wedding, because she did not like this geeky tall man with spectacles.

Another reason why my Mom so resented my Grandfather was because he hid the doctor's love letters to

----

my Mom for her own good. My Mom found out the truth after my Grandfather moved in with my parents. I saw the handsome boyfriend's photo many times later, and was amazed that my Father was never jealous of him.

In fact, my Grandfather had been waiting for the Chiang Kai Shek government to retaliate against mainland China. He did not want to work for the communist government. So, he got married again and had another daughter, lived on selling his personal effects during the years since the communist takeover. Then the new wife divorced him. I only saw the daughter, Mass[13], twice in my life. Once was when she needed to find a job, and came to my Father; the second time was at my Grandfather's funeral. In fact, I did not realize she was my Mom's half sister, since she was just a few years older than my eldest brother History. Mass's mom, Wise, was a high school teacher in Nan

---

[13] Mass for people, not the mass for physics.

Kai High School, an elite high school in Chongqing. She
was an elegant, middle aged woman when I saw her, at
least 30 years younger than my Grandfather.

So, my Mom concluded that another reason why
my Grandfather pushed her to marry my Father was that
my Grandfather's marriage was in trouble. He was seeking
someone kind enough to protect him both politically and
economically. Mom felt she was betrayed and resented her
father.

Mom explained to me that the reason why she
fought with my Grandfather so often was because he was
not careful about his behavior and he kept his identification
issued by the old government still and day dreamed for its
return. This could have caused my Father to lose his position and the whole family to be sent to live in the countryside, which my Mom thought was a terrible idea. She believed that it could be even worse. She saw her classmate, a
very beautiful young girl at age 10, observed her own fa-

----

ther be shot on stage in front of the public, due to his occupation in the old government.

Then, I remembered when I first started to attend school and we were criticizing Lin and Confucius, my Grandfather used to complain to my Mom: "Look at what Wang Yun Song[14] did to this country! He educated two future vice premiers[15] and sent them to France, how did they reward him? They destroyed our ancestor's heritage from thousands of years." Yes, Grandpa did sound very anti-revolutionary, but who was Wang Yun Song? I did not get the answer to this question until my last year of high school.

Mom's cousin Wang Yu Li, who was a very good seamstress, lived in downtown Chongqing with her mom in

---

[14] Wang Yun Song is my Great Granduncle who was a high official in the Qing Dynasty and Chairman of the chamber of commerce in Chongqing before China went communist. He was also a successful business man. Wang Yu Li is Wang Yun Song's granddaughter, my Mom's cousin.

[15] These two were Deng Xiao Ping and Nie Rong Zheng, they joined the communist revolution in France and brought back their leadership experiences and ideology to China.

her grandfather Wang Yun Song's house after he died in 1958. My Mom used to buy some fabric for me and let me bring it to Wang Yu Li to make shirts and dresses.

One day during my last semester of high school, I brought a piece of new fabric to Wang Yu Li to make a new dress and she told me that she was writing to Deng Xiao Ping, because her legs suffered an affliction which went untreated due to the imprisonment of Deng Xiao Ping. I thought it was ridiculous that she thought Deng Xiao Ping would care about her legs. Surprisingly, when I returned to her home to pick up my dress, Wang Yu Li showed me a brandnew wheelchair with real leather surfaces, and she told me it was sent with a letter from Deng Xiao Ping. I brought this big news back to my Mom.

Mom heard this and was excited: "Great! So, Deng Xiao Ping does remember my Granduncle. Great Uncle (her father) did not believe that the communist party could still remember my Granduncle's contribution."

"What contribution?"

"My Granduncle, Wang Yun Song, was a high official in Qing Dynasty, and he became a very successful business man later on when the Republic of China was established. He was the Chairman of the Chamber of Commerce in Chongqing. He founded a non-profit school and sent his best students to France. He covered everything, paid for their passports, travel fees, and gave them lots of silver dollars . . . . but I bet, when he sent them to France, he did not realize that two of them would overthrow the government and become vice premiers of China. Great uncle resented him, because he believed that Granduncle nurtured these communists who later turned China upside down and broke his family apart."

After knowing my Mom's true background, I felt sorry for her and began to understand that her improper behavior in the past was due to an unusual childhood and the political environment. She was not a mean person but a vic-

----

tim of Chinese history and tradition. Since then, I always

try to spoil her with a lot of love, as my Father did.

My Father

My beloved Father's name is Together. He was born in 1931. My Father's Grandfather's family were successful merchants. When they visited the town of Zhang Jia Jie, in Hunan, they thought the place was as beautiful as heaven, and it was so fertile and cheap. They bought a big piece of it for settlement by my Father's grandfather and his brother.

Chinese families like to have many children, and each of the two brothers had more than ten children and a lot of grandchildren. My Father was the third child and the first son of his parents who had thirteen children. I have never met my paternal grandparents and only heard about them from my Father. From what I have heard, my Father never liked his life in his hometown. He said that his parents' generation was totally spoiled and rotten, did not work at all, but gambled and smoked opium every day.

Opium, a confection of colonialism, sounds like a normal consumer good for my Grandfather's generation in

China. Living in different provinces, my both Grandfathers were victims of opium. Father used to tell me that my Grandfather had inherited such a big piece of land that if one rode a horse in one direction for a week, it would be still eating their own grass. However, no one took care of the land. It was leased out, but my Father's family often forgot to collect the rent. Or, tragically, they would gamble away pieces of this land. Although this was regarded to be a bad thing, it turned out to be a benefit for them later. By the time the communist took over the country in 1949, due to mismanagement of the land and losing it to gambling, my Father's parents did not have enough to qualify as land-lords, since they had so many kids and grand kids. There-fore, they were categorized as rich peasants, a much luckier classification than landlords.

At least, they were not killed like some of the big landlords. Besides, their family did not have that disreputa-ble identification which would adversely affect their chil-

---

dren's future. For example, my Father could not have the chance to go to the Army school and became a party leader. If one's parents or grandparents were categorized as landlords, this was considered seriously bad when I was young.

In 1951, the Army School came to recruit on my Father's campus. To escape from his corrupt family life style, and follow his ambition to build a communist China, he joined the Liberation Army without consulting his parents. They were busy playing mahjong and did not care anyway. So, my Father studied telecommunications in the Liberation Army's Midsouth Telecommunication Technology School in Wuhan, Hubei province, and was sent to work for the Yangtze Shipping Company's branch in Yichang, Hubei, after graduation.

My Father has always been a doer rather than a talker. He spoke little but worked very hard, both at home and at work. By the time he met my Mom in 1958, he was 27. This was considered too old to be single during those

----

times, but he was accomplished educationally and career-wise. So, people around him enthusiastically helped him to find a wife. I don't know how my maternal Grandfather got to know my Father, but he was sharp enough to identify my Father's almost flawless personality which would guarantee a stable life for my Mom.

When my Father met my Mom, he found her so beautiful he had no reservation about devoting the rest of his life to make her happy. Unfortunately, my Mom did not appreciate his kindness and love. She cried on the night of the wedding. She confessed to him that she just used the relationship for protection. She could not believe she had to abandon her dream life, forever, with the doctor. My Father assured her repeatedly that she and her family would be safe, since he would defend them with his life and love.

My Mom did not give up easily. She fought with my Father repeatedly which annoyed him. He consulted his mentor about how he should deal with such a situation,

---

since he could not focus on work. His kind and wise mentor advised him to ignore her and focus on work, when my Mom was absorbed with two or three children, she would no longer fight with him. This proved to be true. When the political atmosphere grew more serious, they no longer fought but bonded together to survive.

The never ending political power struggles took my Father away from Chongqing three times. No matter whether the change was a promotion or demotion, my Father always fought his way back to Chongqing to be with my Mom, because he was true to his promise to protect my Mom and our family.

He was so protective he spoiled all of us, especially my Mom. As a professional housewife, my Mom never went beyond our own gate. My Father purchased all the food. Every morning, he rose at 5:30 am to buy the freshest vegetables and meat, along with our breakfast, then helped the janitor clean his office and fill thermos bottles for the

---

rest of the offices. My Father turned over 100% of his income to my Mom and he had no right to decide how money should be spent, but took orders from my Mom. Not only that, he always humbly waited for criticism or judgments about the work he had done for our family by my Mom.

Even as a youngster, I felt my Mom was too bossy, and concluded that I would not be that kind of woman when I grow up. I would give the man 100% respect, allow him the right to make stupid decisions, and to indulge himself every so often. My Mom behaved like she was the queen of the house, and imposed her rules that we must all obey without discussion. I believe her confidence came from my Father's unlimited love and pampering, because he knew that my Mom had been bereft of love since she was two. My Father never told us that he loved us, but he expressed his deep love through solid action over time.

My Father has been an honest and dedicated career and family man. All our family members, friends, and rela-

---

tives speak with great respect and admiration about my Father. In 1984, my Mom's friend Mr. Lu and his powerful relatives from Taiwan, visited our home and expressed his sincere respect of my Father in front our family. He said, "It is incredible that you are such a clean official when corruption is everywhere." Yes, my Father is a true communist who believes in dedication and honesty instead of abusive monopoly power. His conduct and reputation is a great heritage of my generation and we would all be rewarded, if we emulated and cherished his values.

Cruising on The Yangtze

In December, 1984, I joined the largest company in town, the Yangtze Shipping Company, at which my Father and brothers were working. Since I was the top performer on the entrance tests and had the height and looks required, I had the best chance to work on a brandnew luxury cruise ship, M.S. Ba Shan, on the Yangtze River. Many people coveted this job, even my brothers were jealous of me, because my eldest brother History was working in an office on shore as a telecommunication engineer and my second brother Banyan was a telegraph operator on a cargo boat. I would work on a beautiful cruise ship and travel for free.

M.S. Bashan was chartered by a Swedish American company, Lind Bladt & Co. It was an extremely beautiful and luxurious vessel in the eyes of Chinese people. So, in another way, it represented Western decadence and luxury.

The boat was 84 meters long and 27 meters wide, with the hull and super structure painted white with a pink trim. The rotunda of the ball room was painted in hues of blue, yellow, white and red. It had five floors. The first floor contained the lower portion of the engine room; the second floor was staff housing, more engine room, and kitchen; the third floor was devoted to senior staff member cabins and passenger cabins; the fourth floor contained only suites, but also had a large elegant dining room, a recreation room, a centrally located clinic and a stylish sightseeing lounge in the bow next to the presidential suites; on the fifth floor, there was a big ball room, a swimming pool outside of the ballroom, and the captain and commissar had suites on this floor. Above the fifth floor was a sightseeing tower. I still remember the large decorative fan on the wall of the ballroom bar, with two smaller fans on either side of the lounge wall in front of the swimming pool.

We had more than 120 staff members and 4-5
American executives, but usually, we only had 12~38 prestigious guests. Every time, when the guests arrived at the
dock, the sailors' orchestra, all dressed in white uniforms,
would play Chinese   music to welcome our guests on board.
The guests always boarded during the evenings. The next
morning, when the boat set sail, the sailors' orchestra
would play Auld Lang Syne on the dock. Also, when the
boat reached its destination, another sailors' orchestra
would be on the dock playing music to welcome our guests
again.

During my first year of working on M.S. Ba Shan, it
hosted an important conference which not only changed
China, but also the geopolitical course of the world. That
year, 1985, I was 18. *The first International Macroeconomics and Management Forum*, hosted by the central government, was held on our boat during Sep 2nd~9th.

The central government could not find a better place than our boat to host our precious western guests, the world's top economists. The guests included 1981 Nobel Prize laureate *Professor James Tobin* from Yale University, and *Professor Alexander Cairncross* from Cambridge University. Economists and leaders from all over the world were invited to have discussions with our top Chinese economists, including *Xue Mu Qiao* and *Wu Jing Lian*, Chinese central government leaders, such as *Xiang Huai Cheng* and *Ma Hong* also attended.

The government owned media says that this conference instructed China how to transform from a planned economy to a market economy, focused on "government-market-businesses," and prepared theoretical approaches for the framework of the 13th People's Delegation Conference in 1987. So, the government could adjust the market, and the market would direct business.

Today, many top Chinese economists believe that people cannot exaggerate the true impact that this event had on China. If you Google "M.S. Bashan Conference" in Mandarin, you will get numerous results. Many of them were written for the 20th anniversary of this event, because the attendees still have vivid memories concerning it. Some of them believe that this was the only real international macroeconomic forum in Chinese history. Others claim that China needs another "M.S. Ba Shan Conference" at the current time.

The year 1985 represented an important turning point for China. That year, the government started to open a portion of the market for fish, eggs, poultry and some other goods. These were baby steps. This means local consumers began to be able to buy some goods without ration tickets. Before, our purchases of almost everything was rationed, because shortages of almost everything was the norm. However, due to the lack of application of proper economic

---

theories,   the growth of GDP in that year was 12%, much less than the growth of money supply at 25.3%. Under these conditions, China almost had a bank run because people did not know if prices of goods would stop increasing, according to Xin Hua news agency.

Years later, some of the participants of the meeting pointed out, although the government determined to engage in economic reforms, it did not know what to do, especially how to curb inflation. That would normally be the job of a central bank, and China did not have one. It only had the People's Bank, a commercial bank which acted as the central bank. So, the central government invited preeminent economists from the West seeking guidance. As a result, they learned a lot.

On the evening of Sep 1st, 1985, our captain hosted a welcoming cocktail party in the ballroom for all our guests. On the morning of Sep 2nd, 1985, the 80 years old Chinese economist, *Mr. Xue Mu Qiao*, announced the

opening of the forum. During the first two days, due to language barriers and conceptual differences between the
West and the East, the parties could not get along. Then,
Mr. Lin Chong Gen, who was the first director of the Chinese Office of the World Bank, helped bridge communica-
tions, because he was born in Taiwan, could speak both
Chinese and English very well, and understood Chinese
customs and traditions. His sophisticated social skills and
expertise promoted the efficacy of the forum.

Our western guests spoke of the price of labor, labor markets, goods markets, financial markets and production factor markets. For many of the Chinese attendees, it
was the first time in their lives to hear the concept that
wage is the price of labor. They could not believe their
ears, because the *selling* of labor was not considered repu-
table, for the essence of communism was the *contribution*
of labor to build the country. It was also the first time for

them to learn how the government could indirectly cool or heat the economy by adjusting the interest rate.

Xin Hua news agency stated years later, this forum helped the government to establish a framework for further economic reform, to wit, promotion of a market economy. However, in retrospect, change *then* was not as easy as it might appear *today*. The central government believed the public was not ready to accept the concept of a market economy, due to the long time persistent promotion and educational inculcation of a socialist planned economy. If the term "market economy" was mentioned too soon, the Maoists might want to fight to eradicate capitalist roots again. So, it was suggested *not* to call it a market economy, but, instead, a *commodity* economy. Later, people described this change as 'switching on the left turn signal, but driving into the right lane'.

The Chinese attendees appreciated the input of the Western experts very much and they praised them as most

----

honorable and sincere in their efforts to help China's eco-

nomic reform. A remarkable number of the young Chinese

attendees later were promoted to important government of-

fices. Among them were:

Xiang Huai Cheng the future minister of the Treasury De-

partment,

 Lou Ji Wei the future vice minister of the Treasury De-

partment,

Guo Shu Qing the future governor of Shan Dong province,

then the Chairman of Security Exchange Commission

Hong Hu, the future governor of Ji Ling province and other

future leaders of the country

Zhang Wei Ying, the future dean of Guang Hua school of

Beijing University and a prominent economist in China

The Chinese had a tradition of mixing business with

pleasure, the latter including sightseeing, wining and din-

ing, and other entertaining programs. I remember a Western

guest complaining to me he was invited for a business

---

meeting on the boat, and wondered why his Chinese hosts pushed him to sight see on shore every day, during working hours. I thought then he must have been too serious about work, but, after having studied economics, now I surmise he must have been so attached to the subject of his expertise that he could not have fun while unsolved puzzles nibbled on his mind. However, it looked to me that everyone believed that the forum achieved great success.

During the evening of Sep 8th, 1985, our captain hosted a farewell banquet and a party for our guests, and suggested that I sing an English song for our precious guests. One of the guests was Li Miao, who was Chairman Mao's translator and could speak in different English accents. Though his English was thought to be perfect, I still heard people complaining about his having trouble translating buzz words for experts at such a professional forum, because he was never trained in economics. I could only appreciate this complaint 24 years later when I encountered

----

buzz words for economics. Indeed, although my husband is an American lawyer and has an honor's degree in English from Berkeley, when asked by me to explain buzz words in my economics text book, he begged me to desist, because it was not English to him!

I really liked our guests, so, even though I was shy, I sang the song, *Take Me Home, Country Road*[16], by the late singer John Denver, for our guests at the farewell party. It was the first time in my life that I sang in front of such a large group of Western people. After that, I sang that song at *every* farewell party *every* weekend until I left the boat.

A handsome young magician caught my attention at that farewell party. 'Celebrating China' was an intern commissar on our boat. He had a square face with a dimple on the right side, a pair of big shining round eyes, beautiful straight white teeth as one sees in toothpaste ads, an athletic body, neither too tall, nor too short. When he forgot to

---

[16] See the first picture on page 94.

----

shave, his beard grew and that looked charming to me. Whenever he saw me, a big smile appeared on his face. I thought: he might like me.

So, I included visits to his cabin[17] many times during my social rounds during his one month internship on our boat. I learned he had beautiful handwriting and calligraphy, could build and play several Chinese instruments, and had talent as a carpenter, tailor, silversmith and cook. I could not imagine anything he could not do, and was fascinated. So, when his internship lapsed and he left our boat, I felt a kind of emptiness, but did not know why.

Later, my Mom visited me shipboard, and asked me whether there was any crew member pursuing me. "No," I said. Not satisfied, she inquired whether there were crew members pursuing the other five female shipmates who attended my English training class who came on board with

---

[17] Celebrating China was sharing a cabin with three other crew members.

----

me. I responded, "Yes, each had several suitors." Of course, the company had picked the most beautiful girls from thousands of candidates. Tall and beautiful were the important criteria, not English proficiency. Mom worried that I might not know how to catch a boyfriend, so she asked, again, whether there was anyone on my boat I liked. I told her there *was* one, but, unfortunately he was gone, forever. Mom extracted his name from me and left.

A few months passed by while our boat docked with the other cruise ships at the shipyard for maintenance. We had ballroom dancing for the crew every night, because during these times, we had no work to do and could socialize with personnel from other boats. Ballroom dancing had just been revived as a cultural nuance of economic reform and development. Like birds during spring, people began to dress in different colors and styles, in contrast to the drab colors and unisex styles which emulated military dress under Mao. Surprisingly, Celebrating China appeared and invited me to visit his boat which was docked nearby.

His vessel was a passenger boat carrying many peasants. When I came aboard, crowds of people gaped at me as though I were a movie star, because they saw me dressed in a beautiful cruise ship uniform and giving directions to a foreigner in English. At that time, it was rare to see westerners from any passenger boat, because they usually stayed in the higherclass cabins and were segregated from the Chinese passengers.

Celebrating China told me that my Mom visited him and asked him to be my boyfriend. I was stunned, but glad. We set a date to meet each other at the sand beach by the Yangtze River in that evening. I was so excited to go on this date, and thought we had much to discuss. However, when I met him at the beach, to my great disappointment, he did not say anything other than to invite me to sit down on a big pebble stone, and tried to kiss me. I was not prepared for this to occur. It did not follow any procedure from those love stories I read. So, I was scared, stood up, and ran away from him.

Since then, I wondered whether Celebrating China intended to marry me although we never had a meaningful date. So, whenever I have seen a fortune teller, I have paid to get an answer. Though I might have paid about ten times, no one told me I would have ended up with him, and one fortune teller told me firmly it would have been impossible for me to marry him, but that I would have my own successful career. I could not believe all these prophecies, because I thought, as long as I behaved as a good woman, he should cherish me.

After the abortive river side date, I did not see Celebrating China for almost a year, missed him every day, imagined what he was doing all the time, and wrote him numerous love letters expressing how much I admired him. Then he appeared on my boat to visit a colleague but ended up leaving the boat with me. He invited me to have dinner

with his family. After dinner, while walking me back to my

boat, he brought up the issue of having a baby. That scared

me again since I was only 19, had no experience with men,

never kissed, nor had sex. So, I swiftly ran away from him

a second time.

After that, he had never come to my boat again and

I missed him very much. So, I asked my Father to put me

on the temporary replacement team for passenger boats,

because, in this way, I might have a chance to work on Cel-

ebrating China's boat, which was the ugliest and smallest

passenger boat on the Yangtze River. Many people could

not understand why I left the luxury cruise ship for passen-

ger boats, only my parents knew I was searching for love.

I worked on a different boat almost every two

weeks, was never sent to work on Celebrating China's boat,

perhaps the HR office did not believe that I would work on

an old boat since it was a come down from the luxury liner

----

on the Yangtze. Thus, I found excuses to take his boat from time to time, so I could see him and talk to him. Whenever I encountered him again, he always showed hospitality and respect, but no longer touched me. I did not know what to do except continue to send him love letters.

Then I was sent to work as a librarian on a passenger boat. The captain and the commissar liked me. They asked me to stay on their boat and promised to let me take one month paid leave every other two months. I thought this was a rare and great offer, so I accepted.

I had fun both on or off the boat. Sitting at the library every day and reading lots of books that I did not need to buy was an easy job. When I got bored, I practiced calligraphy on old newspapers, or organized ballroom dancing parties for the staff and passengers in the evenings. My library was the only airconditioned place on the boat and the ceiling was decorated with colorful lights that changed with music. I met many interesting people there, from government officials to business people, westerners from all over the world. When off the boat, I enrolled in a school to learn computer science courses and received a professional certificate, or I deliberately took Celebrating China's boat for fun, since there was no cost for sailors to take other boats, just needed to flash my working ID. However, no progress was made.

Later, a bad thing happened to me. After I finished my one month vacation and got back to my boat, the captain was sent to another passenger boat; the commissar was promoted to work on my former cruise ship, M.S. Bashan; and the manager of the service department was off duty staying at his home in far away countryside. The new manager of the service department had not seen me for one month. When I returned, he thought my vacation privileges too unreasonable. No librarian on the Yangtze River had one third of a year off except me, all other librarians had

---

only 52 days off per year. He was mad at me and the leaders who offered me this benefit.

So, when I returned from my vacation, he demoted me to work as a stewardess for the secondclass passengers' cabin, the highest class of cabins on all passenger boats. Since I was demoted, I thought, why not let me work for the fifthclass cabins, so I had the chance to observe the poorest people and let them enjoy my service? The manager accepted my suggestion right away since everyone else wanted to work on the higherclass cabins.

My schedule was no longer 9-5, but working a morning shift and latenight shift of four hour each. When I was on duty, I had to clean the floors of the lounge with broom and mop, scrub the public toilets and shower rooms with a hose. Many of the passengers with fifth class cabin tickets had no beds or seats on which to rest, so they slept and sat in every possible corner of the boat. I wanted to make sure that they knew they were welcomed by my service and my smile. So, whenever and wherever I cleaned, I always made sure that the passenger facilities were as clean as those of the cruise ship.

I labored diligently and worked up a sweat even when the temperature was under 0. This was new to me since my work before was always easy. My parents never let me attempt house work and my hands had never used broom and mop. My new duties raised hurtful blisters a few days after beginning my new job. When my Mom saw this, she asked me whether I wanted my Father to arrange for change of jobs. I told her not to bother my Father, because I wanted to get some exercise and experience how the other people make livings. Although I enjoyed making the passengers happy, I did not want to do that job forever.

I thought, if I worked hard, my manager would promote me, someday. However, this never happened, since he did not seem to like me. He might have disliked me because I looked like a spoiled girl who dressed fash-

----

ionably and used makeup. Most women still did not use makeup in China then. At the time, I thought I might have to do that job forever since there was no other option for me.

One day, after I finished washing the public toilets, I returned to the service desk and observed someone lying on the floor. He fell asleep after eating oranges and threw both seeds and shells by his side. I asked myself: since this guy appeared to enjoy himself so much, what spirits of freedom and romance gripped him? He boarded the boat with a standing-room-only ticket, no reserved bed or seat, so he found a corner in which to lie down. He treated the floor as his bed, fell asleep, and looked most peaceful. Thinking about this, I took a white chalk and drew a bed skirt around the place he was sleeping, then, using yellow, a small table beside this outline. I drew a plate around his orange seeds and shells, grating on top red chalk as Sichuanese pepper, and completed the tableau with a pair of chopsticks.

I loved my artistic work product and wanted someone to share it, but there was no colleague in sight. In another corner, an old man sat close to my desk. To break the ice, I said 'Hi' to him and asked him what he was doing to make a living. He told me he was a fortune teller. Only then, did I realize he was blind.

I thought it might be fun if he consented to predict my future. I particularly wanted to know my romantic potential with Celebrating China and the next step in my career. He had me select three cards from a deck, and groped for my right hand. He then told me that I should have nothing to do with the man in my mind, that no matter how hard I tried, nothing could come of him. I resisted this idea, because I believed if I let Celebrating China know my true feelings, he might end up marrying me. Then, the fortune teller revealed I would soon encounter VIPs to open my

---

world, with great richness in store. He also saw my future career as outdistancing those of the others. I refused to believe this. I confessed my hope to marry a special man soon, and protested that my current job of cleaning public toilets was inconsistent with his glorious predictions. I made him touch the water nozzle used to clean the toilets, and the blisters on my right hand. He instructed me to calm down and cautioned patience, to wait and see whether he was right.

I did not like what he told me, especially about Celebrating China, so when he asked me to give him 20 cents, I gave him 10 cents. Later, when everything he predicted became true, I regretted my stinginess, but could not find him to reward him. I did not end up with Celebrating China no matter how hard I tried. Out of the blue, right at the end of that sailing trip, I was given a position very interesting and rewarding.

When my boat was reaching the dock in Chong-qing, I saw a tall beautiful woman in the cruise ship uniform standing on the deck. She was the manager of the service department on M.S. Bashan - Corinne. I was so surprised and could not know why she was there. She waved to me and told me that she was taking me to work on her boat. I told her that it was impossible, because I had to clean the fifthclass cabin before I could leave and my Father told me that he promised to the HR manager that I would no longer move around.

Corinne told me that she knew how to deal with the HR manager of the passenger boat department and the HR manager of the shipping company. The former was her old friend and the latter was her brother in law. Corinne did not let me clean my assigned cabins and we just left with concerns that the HR office would be closed if we did not move soon enough. I did not go back to my cabin to pick up my belongings and left the boat forever.

So, I was given the position of the manager of the Gift Shop on M.S. Bashan. When the accountant read my financial report, he was amazed how I could do it on my own without any training. He told me that my job included accountancy because it's like a small business owner handling all the business and performing both the accounting and book keeping tasks. I had learned everything by myself from scratch, and enjoyed this new job. The leaders in the higher executive team of the cruise line suggested the shop managers from the other boats visit my shop to learn how it should be done.

When I returned to the luxury environment again and compared it to my life on the passenger boat, I felt lucky that I had such a Father, though he had not done anything to advance me this time. I knew I would not be back on the boat without his reputation. I also realized how hard it was for an ordinary employee to climb up the career ladder. This time, I cherished my job more and worked hard, made lots of money as a 21 years old girl.

I no longer heard from Celebrating China, just learned from someone that he quit his job at the shipping company and became a business man. I thought I will never see Celebrating China in my life again, because there was no link between his life and mine. However, the year of 2011 was full of surprises. While I was visiting my parents in Chongqing during the summer break, Celebrating China called and told me that he was been looking for me for all the past 25 years. I asked how he found my phone number, he said that he was at the Retired Executives Management Office of the Yangtze Shipping Company, and the office staff gave him my Father's phone number.

It was shocking to me that he took the time to find me after 25 years. So, he suggested we have dinner that night, but I could not, I was already scheduled with high

----

school classmates and brothers. We agreed to meet a week later to eat fish by the Yangtze River.

He picked me up at our gate, and still looked handsome, confident and young. After eating fish, he took me to visit his company. On the way home, he said that I was the smartest girl he had ever met in his life and wants to make sure that I am having a good life. If not, I could ask him for help at anytime. He revealed that he did not want to use me to obtain promotions before my Father retired; this proved his innocence. He said that my Mom tried to convince him to be my husband, and even used the analogy of Song Qing Lin and Sun Yat Shien, because he thought he was too old for me and those famous Chinese bridged that gap. Song Qing Lin was the second daughter of Sun Yat Sien[18]'s best friend and was 27 years younger than Sun Yat Shien.

Now I finally understood why my Mom requested me never talk to him anymore, because her ego was hurt.

---

[18] Sun Yat Sien is the founding father of Republic of China.

She thought she used best efforts to bring up her only daughter, who was cherished like a piece of pearl. Celebrating China did not give her the time of day.

However, today, I am thankful for Celebrating China's rejection. His rejection made it possible for me to have such a colorful life rambling around the world. I cannot imagine a whole life anchored to one place for a wild woman like myself.

I did regret I could not go to college when I was working on the boat. Later I realized that the years of working on the ships provided me more valuable education than any Chinese college, then, could possibly provide, because the professors knew very little about the world due to the isolation of China. But many of our passengers were highly educated and successful Americans or Chinese leaders. Besides, it was so much more fun to work on ships than to study in a college which could have confined me to one intellectual box. If I did go to college then, I might never be able to jump out of the box and became an independent thinker, because the Chinese educational system tends to require students to obey authority instead of encouraging critical thinking. My schools never taught us how to ask questions – only to regurgitate rote answers.

Singing for International Macroeconomics Forum, 1985

My Last Singing on M.S. Bashan in 1988

Brainwashing Blood Stains

In January 1989, recommended by my Father to the leader of the unit, I went to work as a computer operator in the Computer Control Center for a vehicle inspection station. Before I started working there, I thought this job was technical and challenging, but reality was the opposite. It was not challenging at all since it was 100% automatic. I felt this was too boring and wasted my youth, because I had become used to dealing with exotic human issues of alive and interesting people, but now I had to face a bunch of machines in a glass cubicled jail, alone, six days per week.

So, the most interesting time for me now was training students from different cities. I have trained several groups of students from Chongqing, Shanghai, Chengdu and other communities that had purchased the same computer system from Japan. After work, I showed the trainees around the city and had some fun. As usual, after each training was done, new friendships formed.

In March, a group of Chengdu trainees came to our unit for three weeks. They were stationed at the hotel of the college opposite our unit and came for training during the weekdays. I found them all humorous and friendly. For some reason, they called me, Master One, and liked to be around me.

Our unit had routine security duty turns. Each employee had to take a turn staying in the office building over the weekend. During my turn, the leading trainee, Virtuous, came to wash his borrowed Toyota van in our parking lot. My boss Mr. Feng saw him and invited him to have dinner with us, so we got to know each other better after the dinner.

After I was off duty, Virtuous invited me to meet his friend, Buddha, who was a business owner and worked for Chongqing Hotel as a department manager before. Since I always enjoyed meeting new people on boat, I gladly accepted the invitation. I went to the dinner at Chongqing Hotel, met Virtuous's friend Buddha and he introduced several of his old colleagues to us. I enjoyed the dinner and realized that the people who were working for the hotel shared something with which I was familiar:

the hospitality business rather than the rat race of a motor vehicle department. They had gentlemanly manners contrasted to the dirty talking, Spartan style behavior of confirmed bureaucrats.

After dinner, Virtuous asked me to play Karaoke and I sang the song, *Take Me Home, Country Road,* which I used to sing on the cruise ship. When the bill came, and I insisted paying, he fought with me for the bill. I told him not to worry, I had the money, because I worked on an

American chartered cruise ship, which meant I had some savings that ordinary people did not have. When he drove me home, he told me he was impressed with my English and asked why I would stay in such a boring place as Chongqing instead of studying abroad. The absence of a higher education still hurt. When I recalled the intellectual conversation of the executives at the Chongqing Hotel, I realized studying abroad should be my immediate goal. Later that year, I enrolled in a night school to review English and prepare myself to be ready for TOEFL test.

Not long after the Chengdu training group departed, about April 20th, college students in Beijing started daily peaceful protests. Thus, were sown the seeds of the infamous Tian An Men Square butchery, of which most Westerners have heard. The students requested the government to clean up corruption and implement democratic administration of the bureaucracies.

Soon, Chongqing college students, in solidarity, occupied our town plaza. I saw buses and trucks containing fired up young students waving and shouting slogans. They too demanded democratic reform, especially freedom of speech. For the first time since Mao's revolution, people who supported the movement took to the streets.

China Central TV(CCTV) station aired the student movement in Tian An Men Square live every day, but the central government delayed discussions with the student leaders. In response to the government's lethargy, the students in Tian An Men Square started a hunger strike on May 13th which lasted for a week and spread all over China.

One evening, my female high school classmate Red and I visited downtown Chongqing to see what was up. We saw the students camped in the plaza outside the government building, and a big speaker blared updated news from Voice of America (VOA). I questioned the student choice of Voice of America. They responded that Chinese media, controlled by the government, was not to be trusted, VOA was the only beam of light of truth and freedom. This was the first time I began to doubt Chinese media.

By May 19th, CCTV reported that the General Party Secretary Zhao Zi Yang went to see the hunger striking students in Tian An Men Square and apologized to them for responding too late. While we thought that this might be a turning point, the day after his visit, 180,000 solders armed with machine guns and tanks were sent to Tian An Men Square.

Due to an educational system that never allowed us to doubt the government, I trusted our media 100% and thought the CCTV was doing a great job documenting the progress of the student movement. The image of Wu Er Kai Xi, one of the student leaders, negotiating with Premier Li Peng, and the image of General Party Secretary Zhao Zi Yang apologizing to the protesters, totally convinced me that we had hope of moving toward democracy. I could not understand why the troops were sent there.

To find the truth, Red and I found the Voice of America channel on my parents' radio and listened to it. When my parents saw us glued to the radio they said nothing, but warned us to be careful when going out. People were distracted from their work and followed the news of the protests. Then I was introduced to a local doctor, Firm Book, as a potential boyfriend. He told me he was required to inject glucose in the veins of hunger striking students in the plaza. He revealed that many of the students just pretended to be striking, but he injected glucose in them as well. He left me a bottle of vitamins and told me that this was imported from America for high officials *only*!

The student movement continued peacefully. Red and I still listened to Voice of America at my parents' home nightly. We thought the students might achieve their goal since the government seemed about to agree to settle with them. However, our expectations were dashed. One night, my Father returned from work and saw us still listening to Voice of America. He warned us to be careful since this student movement was not as simple as we thought and was partially fueled by foreign instigation. He said that the government called him into a meeting where he was told the student movement was simple exploitation by foreign interests.

The morning after my Father's warning, June 4th, 1989, the troops 'cleaned up' Tian An Men Square and many students were killed. I was surprised and upset about this outcome. We could not believe what had happened.

My favorite CCTV news reporter, Constitution, appeared on the evening news dressed in black, mourning the students who lost their precious lives. She reported that the central government defined this student movement as 'anti-revolutionary violence'. The news said that violent agitators mixing with the students upset the previous peaceful protests and promoted the bloodshed. Many soldiers were attacked and some killed. The armed forces had intervened to stop the chaos, it reported.

My Father bought into this story right away, because he was brainwashed to believe that the party is always right. Mom suspected the opposite. I was totally confused and did not know what to believe.

Then suddenly, my favorite news reporter, Constitution, disappeared from CCTV. I never saw her again on the air. Presumably she was dismissed for showing sympathy to the dead students by wearing black when reporting the news on June 4th, 1989.

Top intellectuals like Yan Jia Qi, who supported General Party Secretary Zhao Zi Yang's political reform, were now listed as traitors and wanted by the government. They escaped to France during the chaos, along with Zhao Zi Yang's children and other movement leaders. Zhao Zi

---

Yang himself was placed under house arrest and remained so until the end of his life in 2005.

Thereafter, at work, we began to receive documents from the central government about a new campaign to 'clean up corruption'. We were required to write reports about where we had been and who we were with during the past two months. Although most people had supported or joined this movement, now we were forced to lie to protect ourselves. As a result of this brainwashing propaganda, I changed my anti-government stance to pro-government. Most people cannot resist injected ideas if minority views are repressed, I was not an exception. Brainwashing may change popular beliefs and make people imagine that the *imposed* doctrine arises from their hearts. They would refuse to accept the truth of their brainwashing even when someone demonstrated it with bloody evidence.

This is the mechanism by which the Chinese society forgot 36 million plus deaths caused by starvation after the

----

Great Leap Forward movement; this is how we forgot our

best teachers had spent their most valuable youth in jails, or

communing with cows; this is how we forgot the truth of

the Tian An Men massacre. However, we never forgot the

Opium War, nor Nanking Massacre. We only remember

what the government wants us to remember.

Saving A Boyfriend From An 8 Year

Jail Sentence

In September 1989, my colleague brought me a copy of the Sichuan Daily, the provincial newspaper which reported that Chengdu's Procuratorate arrested some corrupted policemen for taking bribes. One of them was Virtuous, the individual who admired my English singing and encouraged me to study abroad. We felt so sorry for Virtuous, because he was friendly to all of us and corruption was, to us, business as usual. We were used to it. So, my workmates did not feel that he was terribly guilty and had sympathy for him.

I called Virtuous's friend Buddha and told him about this news. He invited me to have dinner with his friends at the Chongqing Hotel that evening. I joined the dinner and people there were discussing the anticorruption movement that night. The executive director of Chong Qing Hotel, Spring, told us when we were having dinner in the hotel, a mandarin speaking man asked him about Virtuous. He suspected that Virtuous had been spied upon since then. I was shocked.

Three months later, Spring invited me for dinner with him. I always enjoyed his company, because he had a charismatic quality that was beyond pedestrian. I thought he had something to tell me about Virtuous, so I accepted his invitation.

In fact, at the dinner, he told me nothing new but repeated the story about the mandarin speaking man's inquiry about Virtuous. He then told me that he and his other two Hong Kong friends, had each invested ten million HK Dollars in a business in Gui Yang, the capital city of Gui Zhou province. He asked me to work for them. Thirty mil-

---

lion HK Dollars were a lot of money then. This was quite an attractive career opportunity, but I had already planned to study abroad. That goal was more important than anything else at this moment. I thought I should not join him since I knew I would not work in China for long.

So, I thanked him for his generous offer but had to decline. He said I was stupid to reject, because if I found someone in Chongqing and got married, the two of us would be able to make 300 yuan per month (300 yuan was worth less than $40 dollars then). His offer would be a multiple of $40 dollars. I did not tell him that I had a plan. When I left, he told me that he bought some women's clothes from Taiwan for his colleagues in the hotel, and he offered some of them to me. I declined, but accepted a small glass jar of Taiwanese pickled vegetable as a souvenir.

Then, I received a long letter from the father of Virtuous, begging me to help his son, because the latter wanted to kill himself in jail. Virtuous was to me a special man among the 20 trainees from Cheng Du, because he spoke mandarin while the rest of them spoke a Sichuan dialect. He was also the tallest of all, about 6 feet, and average looking. He was married, with an eight-year-old son. His wife immigrated to Hong Kong before June 4th, 1989, and she lost contact since he was arrested. Virtuous was embarrassed and felt he had no reason to live any longer. Even though he was isolated in jail, his father managed to ask him who could help him and he told his father that I might be able to help.

I am a person who embraces challenges and likes to help people, so I wrote back to Virtuous' father and told him that I would try my best to help his son. I thought he might have made an occasional mistake but had a good heart. So, on one weekend, Virtuous's father asked me to meet him in Cheng Du at Virtuous's home. I went and met with Virtuous' family members.

However, I didn't agree with his father's blaming the people who reported his son's misconduct, instead of acknowledging Virtuous's crimes. I expressed to his family that it was OK for anyone to make mistakes. The right way to look at it was that Virtuous should no longer make the same mistake after this lesson. His elder brother, Culture, heard me and complimented me for having good insight and attitude. He criticized his father spoiling Virtuous, encouraging loose moral standards. Virtuous's mother fell in love with me right away, maybe because she missed her son so much and had met someone who cared about her son. She also told me that Virtuous's wife, Peace, was arrogant and never respected her as her as a mother in law. One time, when she was cleaning their floor, Peace told her that the way she was doing it was wrong. She grabbed the mop from her mother in law, showed her how she should clean the floor, and told her to do it exactly the way she wanted.

After meeting his family, I wrote a letter to Virtuous to express my concern and friendship. And I told him that I would try my best to help. He was very grateful and became more and more emotionally dependent on me. In the spring of 1990, he was sentenced to jail for 20 years. Virtuous wanted to kill himself again. I comforted him and assured him that we would get him out of jail before that. His parents and I continued working with lawyers and friends. With great effort, we eventually reduced the sentence to 10 years. Then we were told that we'd better seek other ways to reduce these 10 years, instead of going through the court. Virtuous took bribes worth 40,000 yuan, which was about the equivalent of $5,000 then. This represented a substantial offense, but 10 years of jail still sounded excessive.

In case Virtuous might commit suicide in jail, I promised his parents that I would write him every week and would visit him as often as I could. So, with the assistance from a friend, Virtuous was transferred to a jail that served

----

as an inmate-printing house in downtown Chengdu, Sichuan province. It was about 30 minutes' distance by car from his family home in the center of Chengdu, but I had to take an over night train to visit him from Chongqing.

For the first three months after the trial, I visited him in jail every month but wrote to him every week. Maybe, the time and energy that I devoted to comfort and encourage him was too much. Taking care of his emotional needs became my habit, and I could not develop any relationship with other young men. So, when he told me that his wife would never reconcile, he started hitting his head on the wall. I told him that he still had me.

Thereafter, our letters became love letters and I began visiting him every week. Every Saturday evening, I took the 9:59 pm train from Chongqing and arrived Chengdu at 7:59 am on Sunday morning. I had always visited his parents and his son Coco first, then brought whatever his parents made for him as a shared lunch. After lunch, I took

----

Coco to have some fun in the Children's Palace then took him home to help with his homework until I had to catch the 9:59 pm train back to Chongqing. Poor little Coco had no parenting for over one year and became more and more attached to me. He kissed me whenever he got a chance, even kowtowed to me. He begged me to bring him to my classmate's party. He clung to me whenever I had to leave for Chongqing.

Sometimes, I was too late to purchase a sleeper on the train back to Chongqing, and had to do laps around the train overnight, walking to work directly from the train station. My parents noticed this change and became very worried about me. They knew me well enough to know that if they tried to stop me, it would spur me on. So, all they could do was just wait for me to come to my sense.

I commuted to the jail for a year and a half, almost every week. The jail policemen were very touched and became my friends. They even let Virtuous have his own office for proofreading, and we cooked dumplings in this im-

provised kitchen. Incredibly, I lost my virginity in that jail

office. I just felt compelled to submit to his sexual over-

tures or he will kill himself. There was no joy in it.

Virtuous said that he would repay me once he got

out of jail, and would love me ten thousand times more. It

is hard to express how I felt about it then, because I was not

mature enough to reciprocate pleasure. So, the whole expe-

rience was rather a negative one to me.

After this, his parents and I worked even harder to

get him out of jail. We consulted powerful friends how to

manage this. They suggested to use health issues as an ex-

cuse. So, he had a comprehensive checkup with the jail

doctor. The doctor's report said that his all organs were

healthy, but his neck had a problem. We used this as an ex-

cuse and got him out of jail eight years earlier than he

should have. Of course, the process was not simple and en-

tailed lots of help from friends. As is the case with every-

----

thing else in China, the costs could not be measured by money alone.

In the fall of 1991, Virtuous's father told me that Virtuous was going to get out of jail. I was excited but also concerned what kind of relationship I might have with him, because he was still legally married. I knew I was attached to him, but I did not want myself to be the reason of his divorce.

So, I took a year off and enrolled in an English program at Sichuan Foreign Studies Institution trying to pursue my higher education abroad. I still wrote to him every week but did not want to date anybody, although suitors were always around. My dorm mate Jasmine, who grew up in Chongqing but migrated to Shenzhen in 1989, was an intelligent charming girl. She could not understand why I did not want to go to ballroom dances[19] during the weekends

---

[19] Ballroom dancing was popular then.

and why I stayed in my dorm alone all the time. I told her my story, she understood, but opposed this relationship as everyone else did.

However, my thought was still about Virtuous, even though I was enrolled in the English program. Virtuous got out of jail in mid December of 1991. I did not meet him at the gate of the jail. The day before Spring Festival Eve, his mother called me on the phone and asked me to visit her in Chengdu for Spring Festival. She wanted to cook for me to thank me for all I have done. His mother is incredibly loving, I had no excuse to tell her no - and I missed Virtuous, so I went.

I took an empty train from Chongqing to Chengdu on the eve of Spring Festival. Virtuous picked me up at the train station for the first time. When we arrived at his home, his mother and Coco were expecting me. We had great fun chatting, eating and walking around the city together. It was a refreshing Spring Festival for me to be with all of them because we no longer had to be observed by the jail police. However, I had to get back to Chongqing. Virtuous drove me to the train station and told me that he was going to visit me in Chongqing soon.

We still talked on the phone every week and then he came to see me in Chongqing. Strangely, he not only brought his son Coco, but also another good looking four years old boy named Fresh. Four of us toured around the city during the school spring break, then they left. I stopped visiting him and focused on my English studies. When summer break began, his mother called me on the phone and asked me why I no longer visited Chengdu. I did not have a good excuse. She begged me to visit, arguing that Chongqing was too hot for me, I would enjoy a break in Chengdu, and she would cook for me. To such a loving and dedicated mother, I could not say no. So, I went to Chengdu again and Virtuous picked me up at the train station as he did before.

Within the hour after we arrived, someone knocked at the door. Virtuous opened the door and a beautiful young woman with long and lustrous hair came in. She took off her shoes and changed slippers as though she was walking into her own home.

Virtuous introduced her to me as Coco's piano teacher, Gorgeous, and she did look gorgeous, with a perfect face and lissome 5/7" body. All of us had dinner together. We chatted until very late and Gorgeous did not want to return to her own home, so we made a temporary bed in the master bedroom for her. Virtuous' mother and Coco shared the king size bed in the master bedroom. I slept in Coco's bedroom. Virtuous made a bed on the floor of the living room.

When I went to bed, Gorgeous was still chatting with Virtuous on the floor. I did not pay attention to what time it was. When I woke up to use the toilet in the middle of the night, at about 3:00 am, they were still chatting on the floor in the dark. I was amazed what good energy the two shared, but did not suspect anything wrong at all. After I finished using the toilet, I said good night to them, went directly to bed and had a good sleep.

The second day, Virtuous's mother invited me to visit her home in Hanwang, Sichuan. I thought that was nice and packed to leave. I did not understand but also did not ask why Virtuous was not coming with me.

I spent four days at Virtuous's parents' home located in the big beautiful mountains. Virtuous's elder brother's family also lived nearby because they all worked for the same large company. Then Virtuous's younger sister, Jade, invited me to stay at her home in Mianyang, Sichuan province, and I went.

I spent a week at Jade's home in those gorgeous mountains, but the ride to her home was tough and long. I enjoyed the visit very much because of the extremely beautiful natural environment and the hospitality of Jade's fami-

---

ly. After visiting Jade's home, I returned to Virtuous's parents' home and had a long chat with Virtuous's mother. She told me, Coco's piano teacher Gorgeous told her not to iron my clothes because I was an adult myself, but she replied to Gorgeous that she was treating me as her own daughter and enjoying taking care of me. It is only as I write this memoir today, memories, doubts, self criticisms and questions motivated by my growing Western subconscious flood the mind. I realized Virtuous family members were trying to give me a hint what was happening at Virtuous's home in Chengdu. I was literally blind to their efforts.

Following my visits to Virtuous's family members, I returned to his home in Chengdu. Gorgeous still came every day after work. In fact, she was not only Coco's piano teacher, she was a cello player for E Mei Film Production, one of the five prime filmmakers in China. She was practicing for a symphony and always came back with a cello on her back, looking deadly cool. I also liked the way she dressed. Not only that, she was very talented and could do almost everything - not like me at that time, totally spoiled by my parents.

However, since I never suspected that Virtuous would betray me for a better woman, I was not jealous of her but truly admired her. We went to her symphony - the way she performed on the stage consecrated me a faithful admirer. In the theater, I also saw the handsome little boy Fresh that Virtuous brought to Chongqing in the spring. In fact, he was the son of Gorgeous. Virtuous told me that Fresh's father was killed in a car accident a year prior, and the reason Gorgeous was visiting them so often was because she, as a single mom had to make more money to support her son. So, she was Coco's piano tutor.

Virtuous, Coco, Gorgeous and I, the four of us, spent a week rambling around the city together. Then, one day, while we were walking in the clothing market, Gorgeous asked me whether I was Virtuous's girlfriend because she saw him approach my bed to say good night and tucked the quilt around me. I said yes and admitted that it was not right to fall in love with a married man, but I thought our story a special case. It was not a simple love affair, but a love affair forged during imprisonment.

Gorgeous agreed with me, but she told me that we both were cheated, because Virtuous told her that I was his cousin – she revealed he had a sexual relationship with her. He told her that he promised to treat her son as his own and brought him to Chongqing. In fact, I had met her son before I met her, but didn't make the connection, because I never expected betrayal. I thought, as long as I treated people the way I wish to be treated, they would reciprocate.

Gorgeous suggested we both should dump Virtuous and make him suffer. I was upset and took a train back to Chongqing that evening, Virtuous was surprised and asked me why. I did not explain, just quietly left. The trip to Chongqing was miserable. It reminded me of all the things that had happened in the past two years. Gorgeous' revelation also reminded me of Virtuous' complaint that I behaved like a piece of wood in bed.

I got home, crept into my bed, and cried silently. I did not want to talk to anyone. I could not sleep night after night, and developed the habit of taking sleeping pills for several years. My Mom was concerned, but I didn't want to discuss this topic. I no longer called Virtuous or wrote to him, instead, I flew to Shenzhen, Hong Kong's neighbor city, to see my roommate Jasmine from the English program. I spent three weeks in Shenzhen enjoying that southern beach city.

Before I came back from Shenzhen, intending to create a brand new me. I began to wear western style dresses and sunglasses, and got rid of my long hair. As you will see, this became a habit whenever I intended to make seismic changes in my life's course. When I knocked at the door, my Mom could not recognize me, because my hair was shorter than a boy's. I was a shade darker than usual due to Shenzhen's bright sun. I wanted to forget about Virtuous and start a new life.

However, after we sat down for a while, Mom told me that after I left Chongqing, Virtuous came to her home and he had a long chat. He sincerely expressed his love for me and told my Mom that he already started the procedures for his divorce. Not only that, he told my Mom that because we had sex in jail, he wanted to be responsible for me.

He had not told my Mom about Gorgeous, so my Mom was touched by him and would leave it for me to decide. She told me that Virtuous stayed in my bedroom for days and hung out waiting for me at the gate, every day and night. She felt so sorry for him that I did not show up until after he left. He told my Mom that he would never give up and would come back again, soon.

Since I had been in love with him for so long, had forced myself not to think of him, the story of his visit weakened my resolve. I thought that I might have some fault for his betrayal, because I was still too conservative and immature about sex. I did not enjoy sex and knew nothing about how I should react when my lover needed it. For me, kissing was the most enjoyable thing. I felt I missed him and wanted to give both of us one more chance.

Dancing with Wolves

Virtuous came to Chongqing again and I never mentioned the cello player Gorgeous or blamed him. I focused on what we should do for the future. We first decided that he could run a restaurant because he loved food and cooking. We chose to implement a high-end Cantonese-style seafood restaurant, because it had both demand and profit. Business people preferred to consume expensive meals at fancy exotic restaurants, and most other restaurants were Sichuan style except in hotels. This was during the earlier time of economic reform, when most of the economy was still government owned. The government just started encouraging people who had entrepreneurial spirit to charter some government owned businesses.

With the help from one of my high school class-mates Jimmy, we found the president of Chongqing Cuisine Service Company which owned all the restaurants in Chongqing. We asked him to let us charter a restaurant that had the largest space. The president thought that it was a good idea since the government owned restaurants were not profitable and suggested the largest restaurant in downtown Chongqing across the street from Chongqing Guest House and opposite of one of my Father's two apartments provided by the government.

It was a Muslim restaurant and we had to abide by the rules of Muslim culture not to sell ugly animals and fishes that have no scales or fins, such as yellow eels and crabs – in addition, no pork was allowed in this restaurant. The president told us that it was government policy to locate Muslim   restaurants in every district in China for the convenience of traveling Muslim people and pinpoint their locations on every map. If we broke their rules, it may cause serious political chaos - so we had to be careful when participating in economic reform.

We thought this acceptable since we wanted to run a seafood restaurant and it was fine not to sell pork or ugly animals. More importantly, the location was prime, because it is opposite a large four-star hotel. In addition, the president agreed to retire its employees at very low costs and costs for the charter was almost nothing, about one day's revenue per month, and the gross profit for such business was about 70% due to shortage of supply of fancy restaurants.

Virtuous was very satisfied with the prospect of a Muslim restaurant and signed the charter agreement. However, he did not have a dime to refurnish this large restaurant that had a large lobby and eight VIP rooms. Also, new kitchen equipment for Cantonese style cooking required a lot of money. So, I gave him all my savings from the years of working on the cruise ship and borrowed personal savings from my parents, brothers and relatives.

The required cost was about one million yuan and what we raised was not enough, so I borrowed more money from my brother's company and from another relative's company. Then, we borrowed the rest from a bank. All the people tried their best to help us based on my family's reputation and believed that Virtuous would cherish the chance of a rebirth.

We spent two months purchasing supplies and re-furnishing the restaurant. It turned out to be the most beautiful and largest private restaurant in town at that time. Live fishes were in different fish tanks along the wall of the lobby, a huge colorful shell hung on the wall between the fish tanks and the doors of VIP rooms. The exterior wall and the gate were decorated with 'new tech' computerized neon lights that change patterns automatically. Big jumping fish and blue ocean waves would move in synchronicity.

We recruited my high school classmate, Jimmy, as vice president and recruited the chefs from Guangzhou with the help of my friend. We also hired beautiful young boys and girls as servers. The sailor's orchestra from my Father's company played music in their white uniforms for a magnificent opening of the Nine Dragon Seafood Restaurant. The Chongqing TV station reported the opening to the whole city. Hundreds of our guests from all sectors attended this celebration, enjoyed our food and complimented the services and uniforms of our service employees. It was quite a busy and exciting evening for all of us.

The following four weeks of operation were great, with over two thousand dollars' worth of revenue each day. If we kept this pace, we could pay back all the loans in one year. However, things did not turn out the way I planned.

One night when I was sleeping, someone knocked at the door. It was after 10:00 pm, I could not imagine who that could be. I got up and opened the door. It was an elegant woman and I suddenly realized it must be Virtuous's wife Peace, because I had seen her pictures with her son Coco.

I admitted her, she sat down. She told me that she wanted to talk to my Father. I thought it was too late to wake up my Father, but she insisted. My Father came in, roused by the noise. My Father asked what might be going on. Peace told my Father that his daughter was having an affair with her husband. My Father had heard our story from my Mom who had been very concerned about me. However, he was surprised that Virtuous was still not divorced, because my Mom had told him that Virtuous already filed the divorce long time ago. Peace told him that they were not going to divorce and she was here to claim her legal status as Virtuous' wife.

My Father told her, if that was the case, then his daughter was totally wrong and no excuse should be made. Then he apologized to her and ended the discussion. So, after Peace left, my Father said that we should discuss this later after some sleep.

I went to bed and thought, 'How the hell did Peace know where my parents were living? Who could have told her, A friend - like Jimmy? Why would he have done so unless he hated me? Virtuous? More likely, but why would he do that? I could not understand.

I had a sleepless night, went to work and found out that Peace had called my DMV boss and told him that I was having an affair with her husband and requested him to criticize me. I felt so embarrassed and wanted to find Virtuous and force an explanation. So, I went to the restaurant to ask him what was going on.

I walked into the restaurant. Virtuous was not there. Surprisingly, I saw an old friend, Sunrise, who was a doctor and removed my appendix during the time when I worked on the cruise ship. I sat down with them.

Peace appeared as if from no where and walked to our table. She ordered me to leave the restaurant and claimed the restaurant as hers. Sunrise heard this, became angry and told her to get out of the restaurant. Then he asked me what happened. I briefly told him the whole story, then he said, "You should have married me, this bad guy did not deserve you." However, I lost my appetite and wanted to find Virtuous to ask what was happening. I looked for him everywhere, but could not find him. He was avoiding me, and I returned home.

The next day, I went to the restaurant again after work. Virtuous asked me to have a cup of coffee at the Chongqing Guest House, opposite our restaurant. I thought he did not want staff to hear our talk, so I followed him.

At the coffee bar, I asked him whether he took his wife to my parents' home. He said nothing. I informed him were done as lovers, but needed to sort out the financial details of the business rationally, because we owed money to so many relatives and family members. Then we walked back to the restaurant.

Before entering the gate, our bookkeeper Morning Ice walked toward me and asked to speak with me. Morning Ice was an exceptionally beautiful girl with big breasts, 19 years old, 12 years younger than the cello player Gorgeous. They both were born in the years of tiger. Looking at her, I realized that all tiger women I encountered were extremely beautiful. My Mom was one of them.

Morning Ice asked me, "Are you still the girlfriend of Virtuous?"

I said, "Yes, why do you ask?"

Morning Ice, "Virtuous told me you broke up. We had slept together. I do not believe him. I think he cares about you more than he cares about me."

Then, she showed me two bottles of sleeping pills, "I am going to let Virtuous take them, if he does not, then I would take them all."

She looked desperate, drawn. "I requested Virtuous to prevent you from entering the restaurant. He promised he would."

She reminded me of the cello player, Gorgeous.

"Now I am done with him", I replied, "He is all yours."

I now realized Virtuous was just a user. His repetitive conduct proved he was rotten within. And, what the hell was going on with his wife? My heart was broken again but I had little time to pity myself. In China, money usually trumps love. I had to protect the funds I borrowed from everyone and everywhere. Equity and liabilities were under his name, since the rest of us were government workers.

I told Morning Ice that Virtuous had not invested a dime in this restaurant, but my family did, then Morning

---

Ice revealed that Virtuous did not deposit the revenues to the bank. Instead, he stole the cash from the safe daily and no one knew where the money had gone. I never considered such a possibility. Morning Ice let the cat out of the bag.

Morning Ice and I angrily charged into the lobby. I saw a group of old customers sitting there. One of them was Crimson, the School Flower's brother in law who was a police captain of the vice squad. We said hello to each other. I chased Virtuous to the kitchen because he was trying to avoid me. I asked him to abandon his hiding place so we could speak.

He agreed and followed us to the Chongqing Guest House. Before we got, Crimson suddenly appeared in front of us, arrested Virtuous, and hand cuffed him. Morning Ice and I were shocked and knew there must be more to this story. So, we followed them to the police office.

Once there, Crimson ordered Virtuous onto the floor and kicked his ass while promising to pound this piece of shit from Chongqing back to Chengdu. Crimson could not understand why this 38 years old scoundrel, who was not handsome, had no money, was married and had a loyal young girlfriend, could charm the 19 years old sexually awakening Morning Ice to go out of her head over him. I was very confused about what was going on. Facts, falsehoods, infamy, innuendos, betrayals, and financial ruin rocketed around in my brain like pachinko balls and gave me a blinding headache. I felt miserable and had no inclination to face friends or family.

It was late. I had not eaten in a while, so I called high school classmate Health who was nearby to have dinner. I could not tell him the whole story, too much loss of face. I started drinking to kill the pain. I kept drinking, then got drunk and threw up. Health was courteous and took me

----

to his apartment to have a rest. I sat there but asked for

more wine, Health promised to buy some and left to do so.

After he left, my head felt as though it would ex-

plode, and I took two sleeping pills from my purse. These

did nothing. I gulped the entire bottle of pills. When Health

came back, saw me lying in his bed and found the empty ill

bottle, he rushed me to the hospital. The hospital pumped

my stomach and started a glucose IV.

When I woke up, I was so embarrassed I wanted to

leave Chongqing and never return. I wondered whether

Virtuous had ever loved me or just used me. I wanted to

find this out, so I called Crimson for advice. He invited me

to have hot pot for dinner with his teammates. So, I went.

During the dinner, he said while he had Virtuous

underfoot which girl he loves the most. He told Crimson it

was me and Morning Ice was just a play thing. During the

conversation, I was informed the real reason why Crimson

had arrested Virtuous. Virtuous borrowed 60,000 Yuan

----

from a drug dealer, Winter, who was Crimson's close friend, and had not paid it back. In China, sometimes, the police try hard to out criminalize the criminals.

Of course, he said that the drug dealer was just a friend, but the luxury mink coat he sported was obvious evidence of corruption. Such a garment on a California Highway Patrolman might raise some eyebrows. Such a coat would cost Crimson two years of honest income. He boasted he was the great economic success of all the members of his family. Crimson's wife, Ali, was the most beautiful girl at my high school. I tutored her in mathematics and helped her get her first job. So, she was grateful to me. The four of us had played poker cards game together when she started dating Crimson. Although Crimson knew his wife was close to me, he still let me accompany him to ask Morning Ice out. We went to her home, her parents told us she was not at home.

Crimson told me that Virtuous did not return the 60,000 Yuan to Winter on time as he promised. He could not understand to where the money had disappeared. He believed it was impossible for Virtuous to spend as much money as he had stolen in a short period of time, even if he eaten money and defecated it.

I hadn't a clue where the money had gone, either. However, I knew that throwing him in jail would neither be good for the business or get the money back. So, I asked Crimson to release Virtuous to run the restaurant. He refused. I then threatened him that if he did not let Virtuous out in 24 hours, I would report his protection of a drug dealer to the People's Delegation of Chongqing Municipality. When Crimson heard me talk like this, he exclaimed: "Hey, you are not as simple as we thought. How come I never realized that?"

So, Crimson gave me temporary possession of Virtuous for restaurant operations, but had him monitored by cops until he was safely back in a cell. When I asked Virtuous why he was arrested, he said he borrowed money from Winter, the drug dealer. Winter saw the restaurant was doing good business and wanted to own it. Winter's people tried to force Virtuous to sell the restaurant below cost: to Winter. Virtuous told them he could not, then he was arrested.

I contrived to let Virtuous escape Chongqing by smuggling him aboard a boat bound for Shanghai. My purpose was to obtain answers to all my questions. I called my DMV boss and took a month off. We travelled all the way to Shanghai, but returned on the same boat within two weeks. During the trip, we had deep conversations that plagued my mind for all the years of our relationship. Virtuous said he regretted all the bad things he did. He was contrite and apologized. This did not heal the wounds in my heart.

I still could not sleep well, and had to take sleeping pills every night. One night on the boat to Shanghai, still awake at 3:00 am, I took 20 pills over 5 hours and still woke up at 8:00 am. I wondered whether I would still be alive if my classmate Health had not taken me to the hospital.

Upon our return to Chongqing, its environment reminded me of everything negative. I resented Virtuous' repeated betrayals. I suggested he negotiate with Crimson concerning the money he borrowed, although I knew he could be put in jail once he got there.

He still would not explain to me or anyone else where the money had gone. I guessed that he might have borrowed money from someone while he was in Chengdu, and then repaid the money when we had income. Otherwise, where did he get the money to pay for the cello player's expenses? Had he given the money to his wife to please her? I had never connected the dots until I started to

---

write about this period of my life. Besides, my high school classmate Jimmy now revealed, "Every day, Virtuous would go out with Morning Ice and they always came back with bags containing new purse and clothes." Now, I guess, he might have borrowed a lot of money to do shopping for both these girlfriends. Otherwise, I could not understand how such a large amount of money would evaporate in such short period of time

Having extracted from him all the information I could, I deposited him at Crimson's office in the police station, and left. It was my first time to intentionally smash someone's trust. This time, I told myself, I would harden my heart no matter how he begged me.

Diving into The Sea of Commerce

In fact, at the time I decided to leave Virtuous in the hands of the police, I also decided to leave him and Chongqing forever. Once I dropped him at Crimson's police office, I went to Buddha's office and asked him to write a recommendation letter to help me get a job in Guangzhou.

Buddha became a successful entrepreneur running a telecommunication firm using foreign investment. I could not stop my tears when telling him what happened, because he was the closest observer of my struggle. He was always generous and friendly to me, and wrote me a letter to his Hong Kong friend, Hero, requesting he use best efforts to find me a job.

I called my boss in the DMV and told him that I needed one year off due to personal issues. He understood me and granted leave. Armed with Buddha's recommendation I flew to Guangzhou the next day.

In Guangzhou, I visited Buddha's Hong Kong friend, Hero. I knew him when he was the executive manager of the Jade Restaurant in Chongqing Hotel. Now he was the president of a big restaurant in a hotel in Guangzhou. I told Hero I would do any honest work, even become a waitress in his hotel. He said that I might not like that position, because their waitresses had to kneel down when serving guests. "Such a proud princess should never kneel down for anyone," he said. I suspected he was right. So, I asked him to canvas his friends as to whom might need an office clerk.

Two days later, Hero called me on the phone and told me that a Hong Kong boss, Honor, was coming to his hotel to have dinner. Hero told Honor that I was looking for

----

a job, so Honor would interview me at the dinner. At this interview, Honor suggested I become an assistant to the president of his firm, which designed commercial kitchens. I did not know whether I could do it but would give it a try. During the dinner, I told them my sad story and asked if either of them would buy my restaurant in Chongqing, or knew of anyone who would buy it. They told me they would make inquiries and get back to me.

Right after the dinner, my new boss Honor asked me to pick up his briefcase and walk after him. I thanked Hero and followed Honor to his office at the Victory Hotel in Shamian, Guangzhou. The office was a suite in a four-star hotel. Honor gave me the keys for the suite, but told me that I had to find my own apartment as soon as possible because he had to use it when he came back from Hong Kong. He came to Guangzhou about once a month.

The second morning, Honor took me to his factory in the Fongchun district. I met the president, Mr. Yang, his

----

staff, and toured the plant. All of them spoke Cantonese which I could not understand. After lunch, I followed president Yang and Honor to meet with one of the clients. We spent the whole afternoon in the traffic and had business a dinner.

The restaurant was huge, crowded, and owned by the Army with many floors of VIP rooms. After being introduced to the president of the restaurant Mr. Chen, I was ordered to deliver the architectural plans to the clients. I was also introduced to the head of the Environment Bureau of Guangdong Province by President Yang. I worked hard and learned fast. I paid no attention to anything else but my work.

One night, my boss Honor came to Guangzhou and asked me to have dinner with him and his brother in law. Honor introduced me to his brother in law and told him that he wanted me to be a sales manager. His brother in law responded quickly, "Bad idea!" He explained that a young girl was not suitable for sales because this work required much travel. I loved travel, so it was no problem for me. We had a pleasant dinner together. It was my first time to eat pangolin, an animal that feeds on ants and was illegal to eat. I did not know that this dinner contained the seeds for future conflict.

A few days later, Honor's wife visited our office and I was called to meet with her. When I got into the office, she told me to give her the keys. I gave them to her and heard her say something in Cantonese that I could not understand. After she left, President Yang told me that she used dirty language concerning me. He said that Honor's wife was afraid of losing her husband and suspicious of all young good-looking women working around her husband. He knew I was not the kind of girl that she should suspect. In fact, he knew that Honor was in love with another young girl, Si Si, from the Chongqing Hotel, because he was told to mail money to Si Si every month.

I was upset about this situation and said that I would quit. President Yang told Honor's wife that she might lose a competent employee who may generate millions of dollars in revenue. He persuaded her that Ms. Deng was not interested in her husband. Then she asked Mr. Yang to beg my forgiveness, so I forgave her and stayed.

Since Honor's wife agreed to trust me, I was permitted to travel with Honor to Chongqing for a project. I was excited about this trip, because Honor would also check out our restaurant for potential buyers. When I called my Mom on phone to tell her that I was coming home, she told me that Virtuous sent her a letter telling her that he was in jail again and begged her to send him a quilt.

Chongqing was extremely cold and humid in December. I could not imagine how to survive for a single night without a quilt. My Mom did not understand why Virtuous was in jail again, but pitied him and brought a quilt to the jail. Surprisingly, when she asked to visit Virtuous, the jail police told her that there was no such person by this name incarcerated. After displaying his letter, the jailer accepted the quilt but did not let her see Virtuous. Later, my second brother Banyan told me that his cop friend told him, "Virtuous was put in jail under the name of a murder suspect." I became worried.

When I arrived in Chongqing, I called Crimson and asked him where Virtuous was.

Crimson said, "He is not with me but with Winter."

"Where is Winter? I brought a Hong Kong buyer to see the restaurant and we need to talk to Virtuous since he has the legal right to sign the contract of sale."

Crimson said, "Winter is in a suite at the Chongqing Guest House."

I found their room number from the front desk and went there. When I rang the bell, a young man opened the door. I walked through the door and saw two young men injecting each other. This was the first time I encountered the use of

----

hard drugs and did not know they were injecting heroine. I
thought they were sick and did not want to go to a hospital.
I said to the two boys, "Hey, you should not do this by
yourself, go to a hospital." They did not respond to me. I
walked into the bedroom where Virtuous and Winter were
watching TV.

I said to Winter, "I have to take Virtuous to meet with the
potential buyer from Hong Kong."

Winter shrugged, "OK", he said.

Then he barked an order at the drug addicts, "You two follow them!"

Virtuous, Honor and I had dinner at the Jade Restaurant in the Chongqing Hotel. We discussed potential
purchase of the restaurant and enjoyed our meal. Then one
of the young drug addicts tapped Virtuous on the shoulder
and asked him to leave the table. Virtuous left with the addict, and in a few minutes a security guard came in and informed us two men were beating up our guest. When we

went out, Virtuous was being repeatedly kicked on the back and stomach by the two drug addicts, but he did not strike back. I insisted the addicts stop beating him, and they took him away.

Since I was worried that they might kill Virtuous, I asked my two brothers to help. They came with me, and we decided to get Virtuous out of Chongqing and let my brother History run the restaurant. I rang the bell once more, and the door was opened by one of the two addicts. We walked in, Winter was lying in bed watching TV. I informed Winter that Virtuous had to negotiate with my potential buyer and we took him away again. Winter did not ask the two addicts to follow this time, I wondered why. We took Virtuous to History's home, then Virtuous wrote an authorization letter for History to be able to sell the restaurant.

The second day, at our own restaurant, my boss Honor and I met with the beautiful young girl Si Si who was Honor's girlfriend for many years. She came with her new boyfriend Mr. Wang who was starting a restaurant in the tallest building of Chongqing. His restaurant was named the Grand Magnate and he asked us to build the kitchen for him. Si Si's boyfriend Mr. Wang was young and handsome. I could not understand why she later dumped him, and went with my boss who was less than average looking, married with three kids, and much older than she was. That evening, Virtuous and I left Chongqing with Honor. Honor lost interest in purchasing our restaurant with the complications it presented.

In Guangzhou, Virtuous had to stay with me, for he had no money and had to depend on my income. I told him to try to find a job. He tried, with no luck. Since he had nothing meaningful to do, he began to make trouble for me. He began to suspect every man I knew as a competitor, and proved ready to fight them. Until then, I had not realized that Virtuous was a person who would always cause trouble.

My work schedule became more and more busy. Virtuous complained it was hard for too little income and he barely saw me. He suggested I ask my boss for a commission plus salary. Honor agreed and said I would receive 5% commission for each commercial kitchen project I secured.

When the Spring Festival came, most of the migrants returned to the countryside for the long holidays. Virtuous and I decided to go to Shenyang, Liao Ning province to visit his elder sister's family, because I had never seen a real snow-covered city in my life before then. I borrowed some money from the company and told them that I was going to Shenyang for the holidays but also to see whether there were any hotels under construction there. President Yang told me if I found potential clients, I did not have to come back and should stay there. The office would mail me expenses as requested.

We landed in Shenyang one day before the Spring Festival Eve. On the way to Virtuous' sister Bell's home, I saw numerous chimneys and piles of black stuff along both sides of the roads. The temperature of this place was -11°F; I thought the weather was cold enough that people had to pile coal near the buildings to secure the supply. My presumption was wrong: the piles were not coal but snow covered with dirt from burning coal.

The family gathering was amazingly   pleasant. Virtuous' elder sister Bell and her family members were wonderful people, loving and caring. They had many friends. To save money, we stayed at their home. They gave us their master bedroom, while they slept on the floor of the living room. I felt sorry for this, but they insisted. However, we wanted to stay there to see whether there were any business opportunities and we should not let them sleep on the floor for long. So, later we found a cheap hotel nearby and made a good deal with the manager. It was just across the street from Bell's home, a convenient commute.

Bell and her husband, Culture, had one daughter Rose, a sweet and diligent student in high school. Culture was the president and chairman of the board of a government owned entity that was in the fire extinguishing system business. They all knew that Virtuous had gone to jail and had no job, but still welcomed him and I as their guests. Virtuous asked Culture, Bell's husband, what business they could do together. Culture replied that he would rather do business with me instead.

So, to help my business, Culture set up a grand dinner and invited a dozen friends to his home to enjoy some time with us. His friends were fantastic, smart, humorous, and playful too. They invented numerous excuses to make people drink alcohol. For example, one guest cited an ancient idiom: *"Having friends from far away, should not we be happy?"* Then he toasted for new friends from far away.

If we did not drink, he would claim we were not treating him as a friend. If we did not drink 'bottoms up', he would say: *"Shallow feelings, just take a sip",* which translates as we did not take him as a serious friend. However, they made me swallow a big glass of distilled spirit and three big bottles of beer, which made me fall asleep at the table before the guests left.

When I saw these same people again at another dinner hosted by Culture's company, they complimented me a grounded person. They would take care of me, and help nurture my business. After that, I did not have to drink too much because they were convinced of my sincerity.

After the Spring Festival of 1993, Culture's sales manager brought me to a project cite in Shenyang, Gloria Plaza, then under construction. This project was developed by the army, and the chairman of the board was Commander Huang. His father was the first party secretary of Liao-ning province who participated in the famous Red Army's Long March with Chairman Mao.

After I introduced myself to the battalion commander, Wang, he I speak to Commander Huang directly. So, I was brought to Commander Huang's office and was welcomed by him. His office was large enough to make a visitor feel extremely small and unimportant. However, commander Huang thanked me for coming from so far to represent our company and its products. This welcome of far away guests had to do with the fact that travel had been restricted in China since 1949. People could not travel far without the national ration tickets for food until 1993. I was, therefore, to them, more of a precious guest than a potential supplier.

After that first meeting, I invited Commander Huang to have dinner at the Hong Kong Gourmet Restaurant in town. Of course, he came with a coterie of attendants. We became true friends, because from then on, he insisted on dining at more modest restaurants.

To reciprocate the friendship from Commander Huang, Culture and his people, I made Sichuan Style sausages from scratch. I had my Father send me the casings for sausages and bought all spices that I could get from the local market. I made ten kilograms of my style of Sichuan Sausage without following any recipe. I did not have a chance to taste them before they were given away. Fortunately, all the recipients gave high compliments.

Commander Huang told me that his family had received many kinds of sausages as gifts for the Spring Festival. His mother told him that the dark colored sausages tasted the best among all. Those were made by me. I was so proud of my first achievement as a cook because I had never cooked anything except fast noodles before. Now, I found new confidence from making sausages and began to believe that I could do anything if I wanted to.

Since the sausages were such a hit, our business relationship developed smoothly. We had only two competitors, one smaller than our company and the other the industry leader. The industry leader was harder to overcome, but their prices were way higher than ours. Their interaction with the Commander was not as close as ours although it was introduced by a friend of the Commander's son. So, before the commander found the money to finish the interior decoration, I guess he made up his mind that he would do business with me once he raised the money.

Then, I was introduced to another project in Dalian by one of Culture's executives. This project was owned by the Dalian Branch of China Construction Bank. I visited the project office and introduced myself to the Purchasing Manager, Li. Manager Li told me that I was too late since they had already decided to give the project to the industry leader to build. I offered a presentation for their future options and he agreed.

I guess he let me do the presentation because it was hard for him to reject someone who had traveled from so far away. After my presentation, I gave him my business card and told him that I was staying at the hotel nearby and would welcome further inquiry about our company at any time. He took my card and pleasantly walked me to the gate.

Walking out of his office, I was disappointed. I decided to enjoy Dalian's seafood and beautiful scenery while I search for new business. The weather was great with a gorgeous blue sky. The bright sun showered me with its rays and bestowed a glowing golden halo on the red fox cape I wore that day.

While I was walking into a restaurant for lunch, a middle-aged woman patted me on my shoulder.
She said to me, "You must pick three cards from the deck, because I saw a golden ring about you when you were walking into the restaurant. You must have great fortune

----

ahead." I knew it was probably a fortuneteller's trick to make money, but still took three cards for fun.

She said, "The three cards told me that you will meet a powerful person this year, a flood of money is coming to your way, and you will have a healthy and happy family life."

I did not believe her because I was just rejected by a potential client. Who would bring me a powerful figure to help me? No way. However, for her good wishes, I still gave her five Yuan and left.

She restated, "All that is predicted will come true whether you believe me or not."

After lunch, I toured the beach with Culture's colleagues, then we retired to the hotel. After I fell asleep exhausted on my bed, the phone rang. It was the Purchasing Manager Li from the hotel under development I had met that morning. What a surprise! I would never dream that he would call me back. Manager Li invited me for a talk at his

---

office. I met him and his wife there, they offered me an opportunity to win the contract if I followed their requirements.

The couple welcomed me and I thanked him for his reconsideration of our company.

Manager Li, "I never doubted that your company can make high quality equipment."

His wife asked, "How much commission we may receive if we give you the project?"

My boss Honor never prepared me for this possibility; all I knew was my commission would be 5%.

So, I told her, "You need to negotiate with my boss in person. I would love to arrange that."

The wife said, "I like your taste of clothing, let's do shopping together someday."

That was easy, Shenzhen had lots of beautiful clothes and I would like to do more shopping there too. I called my boss the second day. He said that he would like

----

to invite the couple to visit our factory in Guangzhou and our projects in Shenzhen.

So, I gave my feedback to Manager Li and he accepted the invitation. He and his wife went to Guangzhou with me. He met my boss Honor and visited our office at the Victoria Hotel, but not the factory. I showed them the hotel projects in Shenzhen and Guangzhou, and did some shopping with his wife.

At the Shangri-La Hotel coffee shop in Shenzhen, Manager Li told me that he decided to do business with our company. He also asked to borrow $40,000 Hong Kong dollars from my boss when he and his president traveled to Hong Kong and Singapore a month later. I passed this message to my boss Honor and he agreed. So, after Manger Li and his wife went back to Dalian, my boss, the engineer Mr. Shi and I, three of us flew to Dalian to sign the contract with the chairman of the board, Mr. Cong.

For the signing ceremony, we booked a large VIP room in a fancy restaurant called Wan Da[20], in downtown Dalian for dinner and karaoke. I brought Virtuous with me, my boss Honor was surprised that we were still together after so many things had happened. He told me that I was a stupid melon but he was a stupid melon himself, because he was still in love with the young Chongqing girl, Si Si. His wife hated her guts.

Honor understood that we both were trapped in our own sentimental dreams. We both knew that the rest of the world viewed us as the most stupid people, but we could not resist the seduction of adventure and the opportunity to prove that we could make a difference. We both would rather work hard to overcome the challenges fallen man and woman had inflicted upon us, and refused to accept an ordinary life. We had a toast celebrating our stupidity, our

---

[20] Wan Da Group is mainly owned by Wang Jian Lin, the richest man in P. R. China.

courage, and for pursuing a challenging life in our own way. Then we had another toast celebrating my first one million USD contract. President Cong sang a song for us and signed the contract.

The next day, Honor flew directly to Macao to gamble with Si Si and I worked with our engineer Mr. Shi on the project site. When I got back to Guangzhou office, my boss Honor did not give me the 5% of the 2 million yuan down payment that my client had paid. Instead, he gave me 5,000 yuan every time I begged him. It upset me, because I could not do anything with 5,000 yuan. Such paltry payment would not buy me a home and would be consumed by hotel fees. If he paid me 100,000 yuan at one time, I could use it for a down payment of a condominium in Guangzhou or anywhere else. I fought with him for the money I deserved, but he ignored it.

So, one of my colleagues, Miss Qiu, believed that since Honor did not treat me fairly I should change companies. I told her that I did not know anyone else. She said she knew an owner of a much bigger company with factories in Singapore, Hong Kong and Shenzhen. She called the owner, Mr. Tang, on the phone and told him that she would introduce a smart and beautiful girl for him as his sales manager. She bragged I could speak fluent English and worked for a large company before, so Mr. Tang was excited to meet me the next day.

When Mr. Tang came to Guangzhou to interview me, I brought Virtuous with me, because I did not want to upset his libido. From my limited experience, Hong Kong men tended to be attracted to mainland Chinese girls. I did not want to attract Mr. Tang and cause his wife to insult me as Honor's wife did before. Besides, Virtuous was always alert about any man who might pursue me, especially a rich Hong Kong man. So, presenting Virtuous to Mr. Tang would be a mollifying sign that my meeting with him was for work only.

The meeting went very well, Mr. Tang heard what I had achieved in such short time in this new industry. He said he would wait for me to finish my responsibilities at my current company. Also, he took the responsibility that Ms. Qiu, who introduced me to him, might get fired for this reason. He offered to pay her salary every month if she was fired for helping me, even though she did not have to work for the company.

Mr. Tang asked me what I expected for my salary. I told him that I didn't want to be paid a salary, and would like to be his agent in mainland China. I would like to take 20% of the total amount of each contract booked as my commission. He loved this idea and offered me an apartment at the factory executives' building in Shenzhen, adding, "Any time you need money, just ask me or my president Mr. Zhao, and they will wire it as soon as possible."

A few days later, I called the engineer of my current company, Mr. Shi. He told me that our clients from Dalian

----

visited Hong Kong and our boss Honor lent them $40,000 HK dollars for their trip to Singapore. Later, Honor lost money from his gambling spree in Macao, and failed to pay me the commission I had earned. So, I quit that job in the fall of 1993, and started my new work as an agent of Tahing Gas Engineering, Co.

Before the Spring Festival of 1994, Shen Yang Gloria Plaza, owned by the army, received new investment capital and restarted the construction. I told Commander Huang that I changed companies but was still in the same business. He expected me to do the project for them. So, I signed the contract with commander Huang on behalf of my new company.

Then I called President, Mr. Cong, of Dalian Jin Yuan Hotel, and asked him how the project was going. He was very mad at my former boss Honor since he shipped only a few units to the project site after receiving the two million yuan down payment. He requested Honor to send more equipment before making his next payment, Honor refused to do this without paying more. I apologized to President Cong, expressed sorrow that I had no control over Honor. So, President Cong asked me whether I knew another company which could take over the project, and I informed him of my new position. He then asked me to go to Dalian to finish the work, and I was delighted to do so.

I flew to Dalian and made another contract with President Cong. He left the equipment my former company had provided at the Tax-Free warehouse in Dalian. Before I made the price offering, I asked him, "Should I include the kick back that my former company offered in the price?"

"No, I do not want it."

Then he complained, "The quality of our executives is too poor, I can not believe it."

So, I gave him a big discount and provided extra equipment as gifts. He promptly accepted and signed the contract with me in his office. He even refused my invitation for a cele-

bratory dinner.

For my first half year at the new company, I made

enough money to take care of the problems caused by our

failed restaurant that had been turned over to my eldest

brother History. I called History on the phone and asked

how the problem of the restaurant could be resolved. He

told me that it was sold to someone at a discount. I felt sor-

ry for my mistake and sent him the money that we owed to

all the relatives and friends. History was surprised that I

had made such a success in so short a time, and I did not

tell him that I had lived on fast noodles for a half year in

Shenyang. If anyone tried to feed me a pack of dried noo-

dles at this time, I might have thrown up all over them.

I also wanted to reward, with cash, Culture's two

colleagues who introduced me to the two projects. Culture

warned me not to do it because they were employees of a

government owned company. So, I bought two Nikon cameras from Hong Kong and gave one to each of them as gifts. They were satisfied with this. Due to Culture's honorable personality, I did not dare mention compensating him. The only thing I did for them was to buy clothes, shoes and purses for them whenever I travelled back to Hong Kong or Shenzhen. I wanted to buy them a bigger TV set, but they would not accept it. I always felt that I owed them, because what they did for me could not be measured by money and I could not figure out what I could do for them. So, I tutored their daughter Rose in mathematics before the college entrance test. They were amazed that I still remembered math so well after having left high school 10 years ago.

After a stressful year, I decided to take a long holiday enjoying the warm weather in Shenzhen during the winter. One day, when I was having lunch with a friend, he showed me a real estate ad in a newspaper and suggested me to buy a condominium in Shenzhen. We went to the de-

----

veloper's office right after lunch. Since there was a crowd of people signing contracts, we felt the supply would soon be gone. So, I bought a unit with three bedrooms for about $100,000 US dollars. Our company wired the check the next day. I was glad that Tahing always kept its promises, unlike my former employer.

During the holidays, I returned to Chongqing to see my parents. They were happy to see me and I assured them that I would not cause them further grief. They loved me so much and forgave all the mistakes I made in the past. I had a good time with them and bought them whatever they needed for the house. They tried to prevent me buying anything for them and kept saying, "We do not need this…we do not need that…"

My business developed smoothly and my clients kept bringing me more new projects. I hired Virtuous to manage the project sites that were under construction. I did not have to do this, because each project had a manager. I

----

gave him this job to keep him busy, so that he might feel useful. He enjoyed wining and dining our clients, playing karaoke, and hanging out with the "San Pei" – beautiful young girls who can do much more than sing.

San means three and Pei means company. So, a San Pei girl is like an escort who accompanies a client to eat, drink and sing. And though illegal, the clients could pay to take them away for an evening.

I had seen numerous hookers in the Karaoke night clubs during my business career traveling all over China. They were extremely young and beautiful, mostly under 20. I guess many of them were under the thumb of the mafia, controlled by drugs. Some, who were not on drugs, would sing and dance or drink with the men. Those on drugs, without ceremony, would let the men fondle them. Dongguan is an industrial town neighboring Shenzhen, famous for its extremely young and beautiful hooker population. My colleague's younger brother once told me that a

----

19 years old hooker was over the hill. I was speechless when I heard this. My high school classmate Yu Yan, the successful real estate developer and poet, wrote another verse about the features of Dongguan hookers, which should be shared with the world:

Old Hooker

The smoke of the world of men

cannot provoke a ripple in her heart

She only longs to make love to an elephant

a strong adult male

two tons in weight

with skin as wrinkled as the Great Wall

Imagine this fierce scene:

her monstrous flood of blood,

cascading over her perishing vessels,

back and forth.

O she has handled numerous weapons

----

sufficient to arm an expeditionary force

She knows well the distinctive

quality of weapons

from different classes

so well

she imagines giving guest lectures

in Beijing University or on China Central TV Sta-

tion

Her popularity must rise above that of

the old woman

who treated the Analects of Confucius

like costume jewelry.

Her direction of research?

Hair, fingernails, teeth . . . .

all the bodily derivatives

and those beyond body -

the fluid glance, the breathless moan, the

----

facials grimaces and grins . . . .

all the non-physical cultural heritage,

those contents that ordinary people ignore

should transcend the altitude of the professionals.

She says she is old

like falling leaves returning to their roots,

but she can't remember her hometown,

can't remember the man who plucked her

from the slopes of a mountain village.

She only remembers a small town called Dongguan.

The empty pools of her eyes

seem farther away

than the Tang Dynasty.

This year, she will turn 20 years of age.

-By Yu Yan

In the winter of 1994, one of the investors of Shen Yang Gloria Plaza invested in a Dalian project, called Dalian International Exhibition Center. I asked Commander Huang's friend Susan to work for me and take charge of this project, so she may make some money in addition to her teaching job. Susan did a great job throughout the tender bidding and the construction processes. I gave her extra commissions, so she could buy her dream home by the beach. She owned a home before, living in a very small studio provided by her school. Virtuous was upset that I placed Susan in charge of this project but not him. He began to indulge himself.

One time, I flew to Dalian to check out my projects. Virtuous met me at the airport - he looked ugly. In the evening, he confessed to me that he made a mistake.

"What mistake? Another woman, AGAIN?"

"In order to not make the woman mistake again, I made a different kind of mistake."

I could not imagine what that could be. I did not immediately think of the drug heroin, because when he saw those young guys doing it at the Chongqing Guest House, he commented they were brainless idiots destroying their lives. I could not believe that he would do things he denounced as stupid.

However, when I said: "Drugs?", he nodded.

He said, "Commander Huang's son let me try, I tried and became addicted." He admitted he was on drugs for about a half year. Even though he told me the truth, I still had difficulty believing it.

I asked him what he intended to do about it. He promised to quit it and begged me to forgive him. I told him I would give him one chance. If I saw him using again, I would be gone forever. I could not babysit him 24/7 and if he wanted to play with fire, he could do it on his own time.

The next morning, when he went to the project site, I stayed behind in the hotel room and found a pack of Kent cigarettes on the desk. I opened it and saw some white powder in it. I emptied the box in the toilet without hesitation. Then the cleaning service took the box away. When Virtuous came back, he looked for the box, could not find it, and asked me whether I saw it. I told him I threw it away.

He whined to me, complaining, "That's a lot of money!"

"I have zero tolerance for the use of drugs, I hate drugs. If I see you touch the stuff one more time, you will never see me again."

He understood, correctly that there would be no money for drugs coming from me.

To give him spiritual support and help him quit drugs, I stayed with him - although I felt as there was a corpse sleeping in the other bed. In the evening, I saw him painfully struggle with drug addiction. I insisted that he had to prove to me that he was still a tough man. For drug addicts, I had no sympathy.

A few days later, Commander Huang and professor Tian came to Dalian, invited me to spend the weekend in professor Tian's hometown, Bin Yu Gou, a beautiful place. Susan encouraged me to go and leave Virtuous at the hotel. The bucolic scenes were extremely charming, but I was worried about Virtuous. I told Susan that Virtuous was trying shake of drug addiction. Though sympathetic, she asked me why I had not dumped him earlier for all the years of suffering he had caused. I did not know how to answer.

I knew that I no longer loved him because I no longer respected him - though I never uttered a word of insult. I believe I became addicted to taking care of him, a habit as dangerous as a narcotic. I could not imagine how he could make a living without me. How would he survive? – and how would he obtain the money to buy food, shelter, clothing?

When we came back to Dalian, Virtuous told me that he had broken the addiction – he did look better. I be-

----

lieved him. Then we went back to Shenzhen together for the 1995 Spring Festival holidays.

One night, Virtuous wanted to smoke in the living room. I sensed something was wrong, because he always smoked whenever and wherever he wanted. I entered the living room, suddenly - surprised and in shock, he turned off the light right away. I did not talk to him, just walked to the switch.

He stood up and asked, "What do you want to do?"

"I cannot see and want to switch on the light."

He became angry and tried to prevent me from reaching the switch. We fought in the dark.

"If you do not let me switch on the light, then there must be a ghost."

"Yes, there is a ghost."

He left for the bedroom, and I turned on the light. I saw a piece of foil and a line of white powder on the glass table. I flushed them away in the toilet and went back into my bed-

---

room. Virtuous came back into the living room and shout-ed: "Where is the stuff gone?"

"I flushed it in the toilet."

He said, as before, "That's a lot of money!"

I did not want to talk to him anymore. I decided to leave him without bringing anything with me but a credit card. However, a client, Prince Restaurant of Dalian, hap-pened to call and asked me to fly to Dalian right away. I packed and left Shenzhen the same day, landed in Dalian. My client's driver met me at the airport.

Then Susan met me at my hotel and asked me about Virtuous. I told her everything and she asked me again why not make a change now. This time, I decided to dump this guy for good no matter how hard he fought for my for-giveness. I knew he would try to cause me trouble, but I was ready for the storms.

I finished my work in Dalian and told Virtuous that I did not want to go back to him - ever - and flew to

Chongqing. Then, since my birthday was approaching, an old friend who shares the same birthday called and suggested go to Chengdu to celebrate his 30th - and my 28th - birthday together. Since I was stressed by hard work and the breakup of my relationship, I accepted his suggestion and we both flew to Chengdu and met with a lot of old classmates from high school.

Chengdu had changed a lot after I left it. Many high rises were under construction. The prices to rent or outright purchase real estate property were relatively cheap. I realized that it was a good time to open a branch there, so we could provide our highquality kitchen equipment to the expanding market, not only in Chengdu, but also in its neighboring cities.

So, I proposed this idea to my boss Mr. Tang. He brought his three presidents, who were in charge of his Singapore, Hong Kong and Shenzhen companies, respectively, to Chengdu. Upon investigating the market, all of them agreed that it was the right time and place to open a new branch with a big showroom in Chengdu.

However, Mr. Tang wanted me to be the president of this branch. I thought I was not ready because I enjoyed traveling around and did not like to be chained to a desk. He asked me how old I was, I told him that I was 28. He then said, a 28 years old was mature enough to run this business. He further encouraged me by telling me that I was smarter than all his other three presidents. I could not believe him, because those three people were my role models in this industry and I respected their professional authority very much. They knew almost everything about this business and I was not confident without their support.

Mr. Tang reiterated he wanted me to be the president and ordered the other three presidents to be my consultants. He told them whenever I had a question, they were responsible to find the answer for me. I thought this quite strong support and accepted his offer. So, I invested 40% of

---

the equity needed to register this company and Mr. Tang invested 60% of the equity needed, but he asked for four board seats to which I had no objection. I welcomed the idea since I could use all the advice I could get.

We rented the second floor of a twofloor building on the People's Road St, one of the two major roads of Chengdu. If you drive directly north, you would encounter Chairman Mao's statue in the center of the town. If you travel south, in twenty minutes you \ reach the airport. The first floor was a car dealership owned by Xie Xiang, the youngest son of the party secretary of Sichuan province Xie Shi Jie, who he also was my neighbor in this community.

In addition to office space, a large portion of the floor was our showroom. High quality commercial and home kitchen equipment were exhibited there. We recruited people and gave them training while the showroom was under construction. My eldest brother History was recruited to help me. On the opening day, we had invited guests -

regulators, related government officials, presidents of hotels as well as our friends, to have a cocktail party served by the Jin Xing Hotel at our showroom. Our guests brought numerous flower baskets for us, which were lined up on both sides of the road. The Chengdu TV station reported our opening twice in the news; it was quite an exciting experience for me and my colleagues.

Almost at once, our business prospered and became more and more busy due to the fast development of economy. Virtuous still came to my office whenever he had time. I told him not come to my office and bother my work. He then began to sit on the staircase, waiting for me to finish work. To get rid of him, I gave him money to set up a vehicle repair business and told him to leave me alone forever.

He took the money and found a place about three kilometers away from my office on the same road. So, I was separated from my 'tail'. Indeed, my old colleague,

Ms. Qiu, the girl who introduced me to my boss Mr. Tang, she used to call Virtuous the 'tail'.

Whenever she saw me alone, she would ask, "What have you done with your 'tail'?"

"Why do you call him that?", I asked.

She said, "He dragged behind you all the time like your 'tail'."

During a holiday season, I went to Thailand with my old friends who owned a travel agency. A strange thing is that, China, still partially closed, required that I be married to obtain a passport - presumably, that would ensure that I would return. So, my travel agency had to fake my marriage status to obtain my first passport, because the police would not concede my loyalty to China was I single. I did not understand why our government had no confidence in the attraction of our motherland. I had to pay my travel agency 5,000 yuan extra to get my first passport, when it should only cost 90 yuan. I should not complain though,

---

because I paid the money to obviate bureaucratic hassles. I had trouble from Chongqing Police getting myself a permit to enter Shenzhen when I first went there. So, I was used to resort to financial means to avoid these hassles.

The Thailand trip was quite refreshing to me due to its unique culture. We toured around the country for a week, but still felt it was not enough time. Thailand has too many beautiful and interesting sights to see and learn on one trip. Its different Buddhist temples, its natural beauty, its distinct culture and cuisine are worth any time spent. So, I made friends with the tour guide, Xiao Han, and told him that I would come back soon.

****

Right after the return to China of Hong Kong in 1997, the Asian Financial crisis deepened. Hong Kong was hit, the contraction of monetary policy caused our headquarters in Hong Kong to partially close. It stopped delivering the goods that our Chengdu branch ordered and had paid for in advance. It made me anxious, because I could not fail our clients who supported us for so many years.

Our failing to finish the projects might cause good friends to lose their jobs, after they had helped us. So, I tried hard to contact our big boss Mr. Tang, but never had any response. I was so worried that I mentioned this challenge to my friend Nice[21] when we were doing something together. Nice was sympathetic to me and asked whether Mr. Tang has children. I told her he has four daughters. Nice responded, "Kidnap one of his daughters to force him to deliver the goods. Do you need help?" Looking at her beautiful face and elegant dress, I was like - WOW!

Inspired by her, I got back to office and faxed Mr. Tang a letter telling him that I was not willing to play hide

---

[21] Nice is the elder sister of my best Jasmine.

and seek with him anymore. I gave him a deadline for delivering the goods. If he failed me, I would cease looking for him and let a professional firm in Hong Kong explain to him the necessity of coughing up the money.

However, I made the last call and found him at home. When he answered the phone, I was so hot tempered that I peppered him with questions. No matter how rude my manner was, Mr. Tang still responded to me like a gentleman.

"Miss Deng, you mentioned so many points, all correct, but only one stuck with me. That is when you said, 'how can we fail our friends who have supported us for years?' Yes, how can we do that? For this reason, I will try my best to deliver some of the goods, but I will have to leave the rest of the problems for you to solve. That's the best I can do." Doing something is better than do nothing. I accepted the deal he offered.

I finished the project perfectly, but with almost no profit, because the bankruptcy of the Hong Kong headquarters and the closure of our Shenzhen factory caused double costs and expenses. I had to locate four factories in different cities to produce the goods that we used to produce in one factory. It was a long and complicated battle. I was relieved when the project test passed in the end of 1998 and it went into operation.

I thought 1998 was stressful enough, but 1999 was a year of a real drama. I will tell the story later in another chapter. This story alone can make a feature film.

In January 2000, a former client introduced North-Eastern Security Company as a potential client. I called Susan to meet with the vice president, Ms. Jin, in Shen Yang. Then Ms. Jin invited me to meet with her and her colleagues in Dalian before the Spring Festival.

Before I flew to Dalian, Ms. Jin told my colleague that her daughter was about to have her birthday and she wished me to buy her daughter an Omega watch. I bought the watch and gave it to Ms. Jin when we were having dinner at the hotel. Ms. Jin did not pay me the money for the watch, but she paid for the very expensive dinner, almost the equivalent to the price of the watch. It would be reimbursed by her company anyway. While we were eating, Ms. Jin said, "The communist party is genuinely strong, we eat like this, and it still doesn't collapse." When she said this, she thought it was super funny, and all her colleagues laughed out loud.

With My Colleague Mr. Mo in Hong Kong Office,

May 5, 1995

Boyfriend Transplant

In 1995, my old colleague from the cruise ship company recommended a beautiful veteran, Charm, from the People's Liberation Army, to work for me. She looked like her name, charming and sweet, aged 26. I hired her as the assistant of the sales manager. Then she recommended her comrade from the Army, Ice, as a part time assistant for me. Ice was also a beautiful girl who was working for a bank. Besides the fact that they both were smart girls, they could drink men under the table and could run interference for me when I was asked to drink. In China, as we have seen, this is a must for doing business. I treated them like my own sisters. So, they liked to stay at my apartment in-

----

stead of going back to their own homes after work, no matter whether I was at home or not.

Sometimes, they came home very late and occasionally threw up due to alcohol over consumption. I was worried and warned them not to stay out too late and questioned them whether they had been playing with bad people, because I saw a lot fallen girls during my experience entertaining clients. Both Ice and Charm told me not to worry, that the people they had been hanging out with were not bad people. They were the sons of some high officials of Sichuan Province, such as the party secretary and vice governor.

One day, Charm informed me that these 'friends' wanted to see me. I asked why. She said that they might want to check out whether she and Ice were good girls. She said it was important for them and might be good for our business too.

I used to shop with my clients or clients' wives in Hong Kong, mercantile heaven. I often over consumed because I have a slim body that almost suits everything that I try on. It is my habit to give away excess clothes to those who close to me. Ice and Charm thus had more clothes than their income could justify, and that makes the Chinese acquisitive mind suspicious.

Ice and Charm told their 'friends' that their boss was a young woman. Not believing this, these 'friends' asked to meet me in person. Ice and Charm begged me many times to meet their 'friends' but I was always busy. So, on one particular day, when they determined that I had no business meeting, they asked me once again for a meeting and I agreed.

We first went to the office of Sunny, who was the son of the vice governor of Sichuan. His brother married the daughter of Xie Shi Jie, the party secretary of Sichuan, the number one boss of that province. Sunny said that his

----

brother was a shareholder of my neighbor company downstairs. I knew the Chairman of the board of that company, Mr. Xie Xiang, the youngest son of Xie Shi Jie. Sunny ran an import and export business and he had a bunch of friends who were the sons of the Chief Executives in the Chinese Customs. Rock was one of them; his father ran the Customs Bureau of Shenzhen and his mother ran the Customs Bureau of Huadu. Since my imported goods passed through the Customs of Shenzhen frequently, I asked Rock to give us a hand when we needed it. He responded, "Anytime." We enjoyed our meeting and expected to have more fun together.

After I met these 'friends', I flew to Shenzhen. Rock picked me up at the airport. The following days, he took me to several dinner and karaoke parties with his friends. He looked like he was proud to have me as his friend, and we gradually became closer.

One month later, it was my birthday. I invited my-self to my best friend Jasmine's home. She made a good dinner for my birthday, but teased me that I should have spent the evening with a man instead of her. I joked that she was my temporary boyfriend since I did not have one.

She asked me, "Don't you have any suitor?"

"No", I admitted.

Just at that moment my cell phone rang and it was Rock, asking me where I was.

I replied: "At a friend's home."

Jasmine began her cross examination:

"Boy or girl?"

"Married or single?"

I then remembered that Rock had told me that his mother complained about his playboy status, not taking a wife.

Jasmine then commanded, "Go out with him, it's your birthday."

Rock overheard this and exclaimed, "What? It is your birthday? I have such good luck? Let me take you to a special place tonight."

So, Rock collected us and took us to an exotically furnished tea house, with elegantly dressed service girls and a cricket that would sing on command. A girl performed the tea ceremony for us and taught us how to enjoy the tea. The scent of the tea was pleasant, the tea sets delicate, but the tea ridiculously overpriced.

I could not understand why, but Jasmine did, because she had more experience from her work in the police. She used to tell me that the tea at her boss' office costs almost one thousand dollars per kilogram. Almost one thousand dollars to buy a kilogram of tea, that's more than an average Chinese person's annual income! Who paid for that?

Jasmine and Rock talked about various topics, from tea to real estate, to the stock market. It looked to me that

----

Jasmine knew almost everything. I felt that I had nothing to do but listen at this occasion. Then Rock took us back to Jasmine's home and left.

After Rock left, Jasmine continued her cross-examination, asking me everything about Rock, his background. I told her everything I knew about him.

She then asked, "Why don't you date him?"

"I just met him."

Then she catalogued his virtues and proclaimed that I should consider him.

I had no special feelings about Rock and was still numb from the Virtuous letdown, trying my new wings of freedom having had the old ones clipped to the bone. I knew this Rock hung out with beautiful young girls and I did not need another playboy. However, Jasmine convinced me that though he had not expressed feelings for me, he must like me a lot because of the treatment he bestowed. She encouraged me to go for this guy.

Rock invited me to a ballroom dance and began asking me about my boyfriends.

I played coy and asked him, "Which one are you interested in?"

"How many do you have?"

"Need some time to figure that out."

He then commented that since I had so many boyfriends, one more would not be much of a burden.

"You have so many beautiful girls, you don't need me."

"You think Ice is beautiful?"

"That's one of the reasons I hired her."

"You are more beautiful than Ice, you don't realize how beautiful you are."

As apparently slow as I was in the realm of romance, I realized that he was interested in me, then I switched the topic and cut off his interrogation. Eventually, I accepted Rock as my boyfriend without formally expressing it. He became my man in Shenzhen.

Once we went to a bar. Da Wa, his tall and handsome young Tibetan driver, accompanied. Since Da Wa's Mandarin was limited, we communicated by tossing dice. Da Wa could drink a lot, so he joined the Beer Competition and won number one award. About 20 years later, I saw a picture of Da Wa with a woman on Rock's Wechat friends circle.

I asked him, "Is this the Da Wa I met before?"

"Yes, you met Da Wa. He was once my driver but now he has become the richest man in Tibet."

So, I Googled Da Wa for fun and found that he married Li Jie, the widow of the 10th Panchen Lama, and became the president of the company he had worked for as a driver before. Then I learned that the 10th Panchen Lama was jailed for many years during the Cultural Revolution time, because he spoke openly and criticized Chairman Mao. Rock told me the 10th Panchen Lama fell in love with a Han girl, Li Jie while he was in the labor camp. They

---

married without formal registration. When the 10th Panchen

Lama died in 1989, the government tried to prohibit Li Jie

from attending the 10th Panchen Lama's funeral, but Li Jie

insisted the public deserved to know that he was married,

had a daughter. Otherwise, how would historians properly

characterize him?

Li Jie looked happy and still beautiful in the picture

with Da Wa. I was glad to know that Da Wa married a spe-

cial woman and became so successful. I was glad that Rock

introduced me to people who would eventually grow to

have interesting stories.

My work was still busy, lots of travel, and Rock be-

haved very supportively to me. Every time, I asked him to

do something for me, he always did it perfectly, no matter

whether it was errands or the complex issue of reducing my

tax rate for importing kitchen equipment. Since my time in

Shenzhen was limited, I wanted to see Jasmine and Rock.

We went out together a lot. Rock always took us both out

for dinner, then sent Jasmine home and stayed with me for the rest of the night. Our relationship was based more on friendship rather than upon the compulsive behaviors that characterized my time with Virtuous. I still had bitterness about men, I could no longer trust them as I did before.

About a half year later, I received a phone call from a man when I was spending my holidays at Jasmine's home. The man invited me to visit him in his hometown Fuzhou and offered to buy air tickets for me and Jasmine. I rejected this idea right away, then Jasmine asked me who he was.

I told Jasmine how I had met this guy at the Chengdu airport when I was flying to Beijing. I was in the boarding line, and a tall young man patted on my shoulder.
He asked me with a very gentle voice,
"Beijing has no peaches?" (because I was carrying a basket of peaches.)
"Beijing has, but peaches from Chengdu taste different."

Then, we boarded separately and had no further dis-cussion. After we landed Beijing, while I was waiting for my luggage, this tall guy walked over, introduced himself, gave me his business card, and asked for mine. I gave him my business card.

He looked at it and said, "Wow, you are in the commercial kitchen business, great, I will find you! Sorry, I must run, someone is waiting for me in the car. See you later." I thought this behavior weird and put it out of my mind.

When I left the airport, I took a taxi to Sunworld Dynasty hotel, then went to work. When I got back to my hotel room, the phone was ringing. I thought it was a friend who was also on his business trip and staying at the same hotel. However, it was not the friend but that tall guy I met at the airport.

I was surprised and asked, "How could you find my hotel?"

"I can always find you if I want."

Then he invited me for dinner with his client at my hotel. Since I needed to have dinner anyway, and he did not look like a bad guy, I agreed to meet him at the restaurant. Before I went to the restaurant, I took out his business card. His name was Clean Person.

Clean Person and his friend arrived at the restaurant earlier than I did. They both were so tall and handsome, above 6 feet. I said hello to them, and Clean Person introduced his friend, who was also one of his clients, to me.

His client told me how hard Clean Person had tried to find me. He spent the whole afternoon, made phone calls to almost every hotel in Beijing, and could not find me. Then, his client reminded him to call my company, so he called our office and they told him which hotel I was staying in. I could not understand why he taken all the trouble to find me that day. He said that it was hard to meet someone so unforgettable and he had to try harder. Then, his client told me that Clean Person was a good supplier and they had cooperated for several years. He also told me that I could find his products all over the world - he made electronic toys.

So, we spent the rest of the night chatting about tourists and businesses. He did not want to leave until I was sleepy. I begged him to leave. I sensed his intention and told him that I was dating someone. He did not want to give up and said since I was not married and was free to make my own choices.

After I told Jasmine about Clean Person, she suggested I go to Fuzhou to meet him, and she would accompany me. She repeated the mantra that I was not committed to anyone and should explore more choices. She thought that Clean Person sounded like a great guy and she would check him out for me.

I thought about sharks and pilot fish, wondering about my job description in this duo. But, since neither Jasmine and I had never been to Fuzhou, we should take

----

this opportunity to check it out. Jasmine was so excited she did not ask her husband for permission, just picked up the phone and booked us on a dinner flight.

When we landed in Fuzhou, Clean Person and his two best friends were waiting for us at the airport. We were taken to a garden style hotel and checked in, then we were taken to a restaurant. The food was delicate and delicious, but very different from any other style I had tried. The Fujian style cuisine adds sugar to each dish, just like Hunan cuisine adds spicy chilies.

After dinner, we were taken to Clean Person's office in a beautiful high rise. We saw some sport facilities there, and Jasmine asked who used them. One of his two friends told us that Clean Person was a retired athlete from the People's Liberation Army, and had won many metals. He said that they had been friends since teenagers. Jasmine loves sports, and was excited. She later asked me why not acquire Clean Person since he had so much merit. I told her

----

that I did believe Clean Person was a good guy and I would like to be his friend, but I did not like his voice. He had a very gentle voice that did not make me feel that it was a man talking to me, I was attracted to men who have magnetic voices.

In two days, we toured the town and Clean Person's factory. Jasmine was surprised that he had such a large plant because Clean Person was only two years older than I was. So much space allowed him to have a billiard table, Jasmine's favorite game. We played many electronic games that did not exist when we were kids. It was quite an amazing experience for both Jasmine and me.

Suddenly, Jasmine became sick and feverish. We took her to the biggest hospital in Fuzhou but every bed was occupied. However, Clean Person quickly found a young and beautiful doctor, who checked Jasmine into the hospital and confined her in a child's bed. We teased Jas-

----

mine that her playing with the toys turned her back to a baby.

On the night before our flight back to Shenzhen, Jasmine asked me to acquire Clean Person and dump Rock. I thought that unfair, since he had been nice to me for so long. After I had expressed this thought she revealed that when I was traveling in Beijing Rock invited her for coffee and confessed his love for her, not for me. This reminded me that I did receive a phone call from him asking for Jasmine's phone number. He said he was lonely and needed company. I of course gave him Jasmine's phone number. Now I believed that what she said was true, and it hurt and upset me.

After we got back to Shenzhen, Rock asked to see me, and I refused.

He asked why and came to my home,

"What did I do wrong?"

"You have told someone you don't love me."

He countered that my ex-boyfriend had been calling me on the phone multiple times when he and I were together. This was not acceptable to him but he did not complain out of love for me.

I then pointed out, "You told Jasmine you love her, and not me."

"That is my style, express to the one I do not love, love the one I do not express."

He also said that lots of girls were chasing him, treating him as if they had won the double lottery, while I took him for granted. His innocent look and memory of what he had done for me made me trust him, and our relationship became smooth again. Or, at least, I thought so.

I forgot about Clean Person right away and never contacted him again. Rock and I still went out for dinners and karaoke games with Jasmine, and I forgot about what Jasmine had said. Then, one late evening, Rock came to my home and asked me to marry him, because his parents were

----

visiting and expressed that he could not continue as a play-boy and duty to produce grand kids. I told him that I would consider it. He then warned me not to take so long because he could not wait. If I was not worth waiting for, I thought, then to hell with him.

The next day, when Jasmine and I were having cof-fee at a Hotel, I told her about Rock's proposal. I thought I might as well marry him if she could not reveal anything extremely bad about him. She then became very angry and told me that I could not marry him, because, she thought that I did not love him since I spent more time with her, but not him.

She was right, sometimes, when we were doing shopping together, Rock kept calling me on my cell phone. I did not want to answer him and kept staying with Jas-mine. She believed that these were the signs that I was not in love. She insisted Rock told her multiple times that he truly loved her, even after we came back from Fuzhou, and, she herself found that she was in love with Rock. She said that when Rock kept calling me on phone, she was very jealous, so she knew that she was in love.

To prove she did not lie to me, Jasmine said that she would call Rock right now and offer to have dinner with him. She bet that he would come right away. I thought it was a good test, so I let her do it. She called and told him that she had time for dinner with him that night. Rock said, "That's good, I will pick you up after work then." So, we kept chatting until Rock called her again. She picked it up and told him, "I am in a coffee shop with Jin Lan, because she came here earlier without her wallet." She asked him to join us, Rock declined.

So, I could not enjoy my dinner and went home. I called Rock and told him that I had made my decision. He was pleasantly expecting a "yes", but I said that I realized that we could only be friends, like sister and brother, no longer lovers. He could not understand why, felt offended, but still said that he respected my decision.

Rock could not sleep well and came to my office the day after, asked me why I made this decision. I told him that my decision was good for him, because without me getting in the way, he may have a true love life. He pretended that he did not understand, I then told her that Jasmine confessed to me that she was in love with him and I thought he loved her too. He was surprised, but the gray color on his face was gone. He became a happy person, and complimented me, and said, "You are a much more mature woman than I expected. I thought if I dumped you, you would commit suicide."

After Rock left, Jasmine and I spent the new year holidays of 1997 together traveling around Shanghai, Hangzhou and Suzhou, the three most beautiful cities in China. It was her first trip to that region, so she was excited all the time.

During the trip, our discussions centered on Rock. She asked me if I would become jealous seeing them together. I told her I would not, just to keep her from feeling sorry for me. She confessed she would be jealous if she saw me with Rock again. She told me again that every time, when Rock dropped her at her home and left with me, she was very jealous. So, I understood that she was in love with him and promised not to go back to Rock.

She told me that she married her husband, because she was working for Zhu Hai Police at the airport and did not like living in that city. She thought that marrying her husband might help her to transfer to Shenzhen Police, which she did and she had achieved her goal. She complained that her husband still acted like a child and never paid attention to family life. Her husband never seemed to mind when she and I traveled together and never suggested they should spend holidays together as a family.

I thought I understood how she felt and had great sympathy for her. Most importantly, it was hard for anyone to find true love, and if this occurred between my best friend and boyfriend, I had no excuse to stand in their way. I couldn't say that since I met him first he should belong to me, like a gold claim. I think that mutual true love is the number one most important criterion between two people, rather than the order of time in which they met.

She then asked me whether I thought she was selfish. I told her 'no' that I admired her honesty in telling me the truth at the right time. If I had married Rock and found out that he loves someone else someday, I may get doubly hurt. If I fell in love with Jasmine's husband, I would never have had the courage to tell her about my feelings. I might just hide those feelings forever and never tell anyone. Jasmine asked me to give her the keys of my home, because she might need to use them to see Rock. I gave her my keys and told her not to worry about me.

When we got back to Shenzhen, I left for business trips again and did not go back for several months. I did not hear anything about Rock from Jasmine, so I did not know whether they started to date or not. I did not ask her, because I did not want to invade their privacy.

New Boyfriend a Pirate Smuggler

In June, 1997, Jasmine might have felt sorry for me having no boyfriend. One day when I was in[22] Shenzhen, Jasmine's old colleague Fish who was the captain of anti-violence police troop, invited her to have hot pot. She asked me to join her.

It was the usual Chongqinese hot pot joint with boiling pots, crowded tables, loud chatter, a lot of cigarette smoke and beer drinking. Another character out of central castings, one Commissar Liu, came along with several of his attendants. They were introduced to me as high mukety

---

[22] As the reader may have found out by now, most of the events I mention happen in various restaurants. Yes, restaurants are where social lives interconnect since Chinese were used to starving and now it is a developing country with ample food.

----

mucks of the Gold Transportation Troop of the Armed Police Force. We had a pleasant dinner playing toast games as usual, then we went to a karaoke club. I danced with every one of them.

After this party, Commissar Liu invited me to play tennis with his people and I went. We were all learners and progressed slowly. We had developed closer friendships over time.

One afternoon, Commissar Liu asked me to lend 50, 000 yuan for his temporary use and sent his colleague Wave to my office to pick up the money. When my assistant asked Wave to sign a promissory note, he was so scared he refused to sign. I could not understand why and thought he just did not want to be involved in the legal paperwork. He explained that it was not because he did not want to sign but he could not write words properly and was ashamed of it. I was surprised and asked why he was so

----

smart, but not good at handwriting. He then told me the hardships of his childhood in Henan province.

Wave did not even finish primary school, because his mother became mentally disordered when he was in grade one. His mother could not take care of herself or recognize her own kids or husband. Wave had to take care of his three younger brothers while his father went to work. After all doctors gave up on his mother, his family had to resort to necromancy.

They invited a witch to drive the evil spirit out of her body. Every evening, when it was dark, the witch would conduct a ritual recitation of verbal charms to produce magic effects on Wave's mother. Then the witch would burn a piece of paper and threw the ashes into a bowl of water. Thereafter, it was Wave's duty to bring this bowl to a remote rural area to dump it into the realm of ghosts.

He told me that there were no road lights and it was so dark. He believed that one day, on his way to the targeted location to dump the bowl of water and ashes, he saw his classmate's elder sister who was already dead. He was so scared and ran straight home. He did this ritual for three years and then his mother returned to normal and loved him dearly since then. He missed so many classes and could not catch up with his classmates, so he dropped out of school before graduation.

Wave's story was incredible to me and I was touched and thought that I would teach him and compensate his former losses with lots of caring. Then I volunteered to tutor him. He loved this idea and said that he would come to my office to study whenever he had time. We made a deal. Later, the tutoring relationship became something closer. On July 1st, 1997, we observed the PLA troop marching to Hong Kong from my window, because my home was just two miles away from the border.

In the end of 1997, the Treasury Department of the central government was constructing a landmark building in downtown Beijing and I was honored to be one of its suppliers. I told Jasmine this good news and she flew to Beijing to participate in our signing ceremony. At the ceremony, I made a toast to thank Mr. Chen and his executive team for their support in the past and hoped we would have smooth cooperation on this new project. Jasmine, again, as usual the charming Leo woman, took over the rest of the dinner as if she was the hostess. Our clients enjoyed her participation, I think they liked her active, dynamic personality.

After Jasmine and I flew back to Shenzhen from Beijing, the long New Year holidays came. Jasmine and I decided to take a trip to The Philippines and Thailand. We took a chartered plane with a group of rich Chinese gamblers and government high officials from Hong Kong to Subic Bay the home of the US Naval base.

When we landed at the airport, a line of long limousines awaited us. Jasmine's sister Nice, was the tour leader of this special team and she had two handsome Hong Kong young men assisting her work. Neither Jasmine nor I knew how to gamble. Nice conducted the arrangements of limousine for every guest, we were given a limousine which took us to the lobby of a fancy tropical style casino. The lobby had an open ocean view and there was no air conditioning. Electric fans shaped like the leaves of banana trees hung from the ceiling. Surrounded by many tropical plants, the furniture and art pieces were so fresh and natural, it was as if we were in a jungle. I forgot the name of this casino, but I was told that it was the best on the Island.

We checked in and walked around the surrounding area. The people were so nice and beautiful. We could detect the enormous colonial influence upon this culture. For example, though Pilipinos have their own language, Tagalog, the written script is based on the western characters.

The surrounding architecture is based on a suburb of the West. When rambling around the neighborhoods, one would not believe this was Asia.

There was a bat park by the ocean. I thought that the sleeping bats hanging on the trees were the leaves of the trees. When I realized that all of those were alive, it scared me and we ran to the beach right away. The beach was so clean and beautiful with many big seagulls were flying in the sky, and few people.

We sat on the beach to get the sun, Jasmine looked at the indigenous people and told me that I did not look like a Chinese, but a local. To our Chinese, if people tell you that you look like a ghost, or a foreigner, it is a compliment. It is fun to be regarded as exotic. I loved the smell of sun and sea. I always was in a good mood when I could see the ocean on a good weather day, no matter my troubles. I commented to Jasmine that such a beautiful place should be shared with our beloved ones. I still had not found a man who could understand me. Although Wave and I started dating, he was far from being able to understand me or catch up with my thinking. Our real thoughts rarely intersected during conversations. He would love watching those communist revolutionary movies on the TV, over and over. My mind reached out to the world beyond. I wondered where on the earth my dream lover might be.

When it grew dark, Jasmine and I went back to our hotel by the sea to have dinner. We started to learn how to play black jack, did not have good luck, but we had more luck playing the slot machine. In the late night, we called two massage girls to provide us service at our room before sleep. The Philippine peso was declining against Chinese yuan due to Asian Financial Crisis and the prices were cheap.

The next day, when I was at the lobby making an international phone call to my company at the front desk, a very tall man walked over to me and asked where I was

----

from. He was on the same charter plane with us. I did not know why he asked such a question, and did not give him a straight answer.

Later, Jasmine told her sister Nice that a tall guy asked who I was, Nice said that it was Commander Liu Li Yuan, the son of the former vice chairman of the Chinese People's Political Consultative Conference (C.P.P.C.C.) That evening, I was told that he won about 17 million Hong Kong dollars, roughly $2 million US dollars. The casino could not believe that this group of Chinese had not cheated. This event swiftly attracted both police and the local media. We saw people carrying those serious cameras running into the casino with more police, but Jasmine and I could not know what happened inside. Those Chinese did not play in the lobby, they had their own VIP room.

We came to Subic Bay on Friday afternoon and we were supposed to leave on Sunday afternoon. I do not know whether Commander Liu's winning caused us trouble, but we were told that our plane would not arrive on Sunday and we had to stay there one more night. That Sunday night, Commander Liu and his team kept winning more money, about five million Hong Kong dollars this time. He showed no sign of losing confidence. I was wondering whether they could detain Commander Liu there since he won so much money. However, the airplane eventually came and we left this beautiful Island.

Then Jasmine and I flew to Bangkok and we spend the rest of the holidays there. We first hired the guide Xiao Han who I met on my first trip to Thailand. Then, he designed our agenda. We toured ten cities from the north to the south and from the east to the west, mostly by plane and only took one long distance bus. Sometimes, we had two guides and one driver serving our trip, because we had to hire a local travel agency to show us the local culture of which Xiao Han knew very little. Besides checking out the Royal Palace, Four Face Thai Buddha, the hermaphrodite

----

shows, elephant shows and the like, we toured several is-

lands and Gui Lin on the Sea.[23] Due to the currency depre-

ciation, we could afford to enjoy all kinds of food styles,

exotic fruits, and stayed in the best hotels of Thailand. Eve-

ry day was like living in a dream world.

I encountered a strange thing in Bangkok though.

While touring the market, I saw a bag that was the right

size for me to do more shopping. I was just about to buy it

but discovered it was plastic. So, I put it down and left. The

owner of the bag stall, who I thought it was a girl, patted

me one the shoulder and asked me to watch her burn the

bag with a lighter. Of course, she was pretending to burn it

and not let the fire touch the bag. I pushed the lighter to-

ward the bag, but she resisted. So, I shook my head and

left. She got mad and kicked me on my leg, I kicked her

---

[23] Gui Lin is a Chinese city famous for the strange shape of its
mountains.

back immediately reflexively. Staring at an Adam's apple told me he was not a girl, and that I was no match for him.

I gave up and joined Jasmine and her sister Nice's friend. I asked why a hermaphrodite dancer was doing business in the market. Nice's friend told us that it was normal for them to make more income, they do businesses in the day time and perform in the evening, and/or taken out by their clients thereafter.

That midnight, when we got into the elevator of our hotel, we saw the same hermaphrodite I kicked in the market with a handsome American middle-aged man. They behaved like lovers. Jasmine whispered to me, "This American man must have been cheated, he could not know it is a man." We told this story to our guide Xiao Han the second day, he said that it was normal - the American man knew exactly what he was buying. He had seen a lot of such things, and it was no surprise to him. Jasmine and I felt that we too naive and ignorant. As Orson Welles famously said,

----

"No one knew what lurks in the hearts of men. Only the Shadow knows."

In Qing Mai, we visited the ancient temple and watched the minority sect dance show and a place for people who would like to place bets on a piece of stone that might contain jade. The infamous drug dealing Golden Triangle was located nearby. We saw beautiful opium flowers depicted in the arts and wanted to take pictures of the real ones. However, it was hard to find them, because the local people plant them secretly. A local breeze carried a smell familiar from the Chongqinese hotpots restaurants. I believed it might come from the direction where opium plants would be found. I heard that hotpot restaurants like to put dry opium fruits to attract customers. Since there was no Chongqing hotpot restaurant around, there must be opium plants nearby. We followed the hotpot smell and found a big piece of land with colorful opium flowers.

Thailand is a beautiful country with rich resources and a fascinating culture. Its government is democratic and open minded, and it embraces diversity. People may do anything as long as they don't break their law. Even if you are an illegal immigrant, the government would not throw you out of the country as long as you don't break its laws. We could see all international brands in the market, even in remote villages, because Thailand participated in the WTO, but China did not. It is a country with a lot of charm. Jasmine even suggested that we should buy a rice paddy and immigrate to Thailand.

Among those domestic trips in Thailand, the most impressive experience was our adventure on Pi Pi island. Our tour guide Xiao Han introduced this place to us as one where Asian tourists had never been. It was the most beautiful island in Thailand and reserved for Western tourists. Thus, we decided to make history by going there.

After we landed at the airport, we got on a small jet boat. The weather was not bad, the blue sky the same color as the ocean. Several beautiful young westerners stepped onto the front deck. I envied them, because it appeared to me that they enjoyed the sun, the wind, and the waves while I had to struggle with my motion sickness.

The further we sailed, the stronger the wind blew, and the larger the waves grew. So, the captain ordered the passengers to go back to their seats, and close all the doors. Suddenly, we found ourselves in the water. I mean, *in* the water, not on the water! Because, from both sides of our windows, all we could see was water! The boat vibrated violently. I thought that I must grab a life-jacket, but Xiao Han said to me: "Don't do that, people would laugh at you." He smiled at me.

"I am really scared to death, aren't you afraid? You see, we've been in the water for several minutes already!"

"I've never experienced such a strong storm, I am scared too." Xiao Han admitted.

"Look at that westerner," I said, "he is still reading, how can he be so calm? I admire him."

"He is scared too. The book he is reading is the Bible."

After a miserable struggle, we finally saw the sky again, but it was not the same sky as we saw when we boarded this boat. It was gray and depressing. Finally, our little jet boat arrived 3 and ½ hours after it was due. When we reached the shore, we were told that we had to take a very small craft which was called long tail boat to go to Pi-pi Island. I was scared to death already, but there was no other option. We boarded the little tiny long tail boat and I couldn't believe it was capable of sailing on a stormy day. After having been beaten and washed by the storm for about 40 minutes, finally, we made it to the luxury resort on Pi Pi Island.

Still, no words could describe how scared I was. I immediately asked the reception desk if I could go back by car upon return. My brain must have been badly twisted. How can people drive on the sea since there is no bridge? The reception girl answered:

"No car in history, and only a private plane appeared before."

In the two hours after we walked into our room, I didn't dare to open the curtain and look at the sea. Thus, a so-called ocean loving person, had the only enough courage to enjoy the beautifully colored dead fish hanging on the wall. Xiao Han and Jasmine went swimming right away and came back telling me that their bikinis made them the most clothed human beings on the island. The rest of the swimmers were all naked. Jasmine told me the fishes she saw in the ocean looked exactly like the dead ones on the wall. I was upset by my cowardice and regretted the chance to observe everything first hand.

That evening, when we were sitting under the beautiful coconut tree silhouetted by the moon and its creamy halo, having our dinner, the storm ceased, only the breeze gently dancing through our hair. The moon hung below the twinkling stars. Romantic music, accompanied with wine, the delicious fresh seafood, the surrounding beautifully dressed western people prompted Jasmine to say, "It fantastic, I've only seen such scenes in the movies or in my dreams."

Until now, we had only travelled to Hong Kong, Macao, Subic Bay and about ten cities in Thailand. All have free market systems. We began to realize what free markets could do to an economy, but still could not understand why our own country was excluded from this system. We came home with lots of designer clothes, shoes, watches and purses. I still bought several shirts for my first boy-friend Virtuous, because taking care of him became a habit after so many years. Jasmine saw the clothes and asked me who they were for. When I told her that those were for Vir-tuous, she angrily warned me to stop taking care of him; it was not a woman's duty to take care of a man but a man's duty to take care of a woman. She had yet to discover sex-ism. She told me not to break tradition, so I later gave all the men's shirts to Wave and his boss Commissar Liu.

Before we left Bangkok, Nice's friend 'Brother B' invited Jasmine and I for dinner. On the way to the restau-rant, Jasmine asked me not to mention the two young Hong Kong boys assisting Nice in the Philippines, because it was important. At dinner, Brother B asked whether I saw any-body else with us in the Philippines, I shook my head and said nothing. I had question marks in my head for 20 years, but never asked Jasmine why. She finally told me last year that tall Brother B was the head of the Triad in Hong Kong

---

and some people who disappeared were connected to him. That was why she required me not to mention the two young boys assisting Nice. I finally understood.

***

Besides everything becoming cheaper, I could not realize what the Asian Financial Crisis meant until I saw a beautiful young girl jump off the 24th floor of my neighbor building in front of my eyes. One weekend, when my maid Lily was cleaning the windows on the porch, she heard an enormous noise outside and looked down to the street. She saw crowds of people gathered together in the street looking up to our building. She exclaimed, "See what the people are watching!" I thought that a promotion was underway, because the first five floors of our building were a department store and it held commercial activities almost every weekend. This building has four 36 floor towers. I was living in the 15th floor of the second tower.

So, I suggested it might be just one of those commercials. Lily looked back again and said to me, "No, it doesn't look like that at all. There are six fire trucks there. Is something on fire?" I ran to the porch and looked all around this complex, there was no sign of fire. Then Lily pointed to a window from our neighbor tower and exclaimed, "Someone wants to jump off the building!" I followed her finger and saw a young pretty girl with very white skin in a beautiful black dress. A lonely figure she sat on the concrete overhang of a window at about 23rd floor.

I was worried and could not understand why such a young girl abandoned hope in this world. The police inflated a huge air bag on the roof of the fifth floor, because it was supposed to be the location where the girl would land after jumping. There were several very insecure nets built around the building. I did not believe any one of them was sufficient to absorb the weight of this girl's body.

Lily went down to the street to find out what was happening. Then she came back and told me that the girl had been on the overhang of the window since 3:00 pm and now it was almost 9:00 pm. God, she had been there for six hours: obviously, she did not want to die. Why had no one done anything constructive during those six hours? Lily told me that the vice chief of police was there speaking to the girl. He said, "Come here, give me your hand, I will take you back." However, his hand, though a few meters away from the girl, never reached her. He could have attached a safety belt and crawled across the concrete to reach the girl. Or he could have found a smaller individual to do so. Why didn't he have this level of courage, or was his lassitude a commentary on his lack of consideration for one human life? I did not think the police were competent or brave enough, and the fire trucks only attracted people like bluebottle flies.

At around 9:30 pm, my new boyfriend Wave came to my home. He heard what was happening from the security guards. He walked to the window of my bedroom and cried loudly, "She is going to jump now, come here, give me your camera, give me your camera!" I walked to the window, but refused to give him my camera, because I did not feel she was entertainment. I observed the girl's final leap from the building, her beautiful body like a ballet dancer spinning through the air. Her black dress billowed like the wings of a black swan. Her body hit the air bag that was set to save her, but, since it was over inflated, it catapulted her off the roof of the fifth floor and she landed in the street. Thousands of people observed her hopeless jump, the loss of a precious, beautiful life. The show over, the people vacated the street within ten minutes, leaving this girl's lonely corpse alone for three hours.

I kept vigil with the corpse of this unknown human sister until about midnight, when a truck came and collect-

---

ed he remains. Lily said that it was a pity to let a girl die so young. I complained about the police, "If this had happened in the West, I believe she could have been saved." Lily told me that she heard someone in the street yell up to the girl, "If you want to jump, jump now. Don't let me wait too long. There are too many Chinese people." I was so sad hearing this and hated the numb attitude about life. Right after the girl jumped off the building, the police arrested the girl's boyfriend who was there visiting his friend.

We heard from the security guards that the girl and her boyfriend were visiting our neighbor. The girl did not have a job and lived with her boyfriend. Then the Asian Financial Crisis made many companies downsize or close; her boyfriend lost his job and could not afford to rent an apartment anymore. So, he told the girlfriend to go back to her hometown and he would continue to stay in Shenzhen and try to find a job that provided housing. He promised

---

that he would take her back once his economic situation grew better.

However, the girlfriend did not believe him and thought he was dumping her forever. She insisted that she wouldrather die in Shenzhen than return home. So, when they were visiting their friend in a tall building, the girl went into the toilet and climbed out the window to the concrete overhang. Her boyfriend found out and called the police.

Shenzhen Special Economic Zone Daily reported the suicide the next day without a picture, Wave blamed me not giving him my camera. I was amazed by his numb attitude toward life. The image of the girl in the air is engraved forever in my conscious. I asked numerous people numerous times why Chinese are so numb about life and death. A Chinese general Liu Ya Zhou pointed out the striking truth that since many Chinese people had never respected their own life, why respect others?

Although this suicide was an indirect result of the Asian Crisis, I felt the declining moral standard of the society was at fault too. During the surge in the Chinese economy, lots of girls believed that they did not have to go to work; finding rich men to care for them was their best hope. In addition, people began to believe that cheating was a norm for men. Whether rich or not, cheating men of all strata make most women feel insecure 24/7. I experienced the reality that every Hong Kong man I met had mistresses, and was shopping for more. At least half of the mainland Chinese men I encountered had mistresses. When there is no trust between the sexes, the only trustworthy thing is money - and the accession to it. How sad is that?

***

Before the Spring Festival of 1998, Wave was sent to a business trip in Chengdu. He borrowed $10,000 dollars' worth of RMB from me and he told me that he was going to spend the Spring Festival with me and my Mom in

----

Shenzhen. I missed him during the long holidays; however,

he did not return and Spring Festival had passed by the

time he did. I had not a clue what he was up to in Chengdu.

When he returned after the Spring Festival, I was mad at

him and we had a fight. He joked that if I dumped him, lots

of women would come forage for him. I did not believe

him, because I thought he should realize he could not find a

better woman than me. I always treated him with respect

and full support, I thought he must understand that what he

must cherish.

Wave left Shenzhen for Chengdu again, this time, in

case I felt lonely, he asked his Commissar Liu to company

me whenever I needed someone to talk to. So, I had dinners

with Commissar Liu from time to time. One day, he asked

me whether I had trouble with any business associate, be-

cause Wave asked him to watch over me. I realized Wave

might have told him about my troubles with one of my

---

business partners, Tiger, who did not record the transactions in the low-end kitchen firm's accounting book. Each of us owned 50% of this kitchen equipment business, but he was the one in charge of the operations. We had built in excess of 20 commercial kitchen projects all over Shenzhen, and a few in some other provinces. The plant had been busy producing products every day for over a year since it started, but I did not see records of these transactions in our accounting book, not to mention division of profits or distribution of potential dividends. The chairman of the board was my partner Tiger - his flimsy excuse for lack of records keeping was that if he recorded everything in the accounting book, I would be able to report him to the tax bureau for tax fraud.

So, when Commissar Liu suggested he speak to my partner Tiger in person. I thought that might be a good idea. Without thinking this through carefully, we arrived at the

----

factory. The security guard opened the gate and admitted our car. The workers were busy producing various kitchen equipment.

We walked into the office and demanded my partner, Tiger, who was busy with a client out of the office, to return. I could have cared less. It didn't matter how many clients he had or serviced; I had not received a dime of the monies owing me. I promised him we would closedown production if he did not return in two hours. He refused to return. Commissar Liu instructed the workers to stop fabricating. The security guard observed me fighting with Tiger on phone and became irritated, because he was from Tiger's home town and they were relatives.

Following Commissar Liu to the plant, I saw the workers gradually stopped working. I apologized to them but expected them to understand my motivations. Then I heard a scuffle from the office, and upon returning found

---

several soldiers faced off with the security guard and the walls covered with blood. I was shocked and asked what happened. One of the two soldiers said that the security guard had grabbed a glass ashtray, yelled to the workers that he was being attacked, and asked them to join the me-lee. The soldiers felt that they had been tricked, and pushed him into the wall, which broke his nose, and from which spurted the blood.

However, it was not my intent for this to get out of hand and I felt pity for the security guard. I took out all the money I had in my purse, about five thousand dollars' worth of RMB and HKD, gave to the manager of the plant and asked him to take the security guard to the hospital right away. Then, Tiger called the police and TV stations. The police came and arrested all of us. Commissar Liu called his boss immediate superior to tone down the press.

The police inspector invited me to his office and I had a seat. When he stepped out of the office for a moment, I called Jasmine who was working in the Shenzhen Police and told her what happened. She said that she would help me and not to worry. Then the police inspector came back to his office, and asked what happened. I told him about everything. He said that he could put me in jail because I brought the soldiers to the factory and disturbed their production. No matter whether I owned this business or not, I had no right to stop the production and bring soldiers to beat people. I did not wish to push this further. So, I said that I was sorry for what happened, and would take full responsibility for this incident. Then, we helped them complete their file, filled in the police log and left the police station.

I knew, without Jasmine's help, I might end up in jail for at least a month, and perhaps maybe years. I always thought it was Jasmine's boss who made the call to save me because she used to take me to have dinners with her boss and her boss's friends. In fact, 20 years later, Jasmine told me who saved me that time was not her boss but her boss's friend, Brother Chao, who was the head of a Hong Kong mafia and a retired Hong Kong police man.

I remembered having dinner with Brother Chao several times, and he used to send his two Mercedes Benz cars to help us shop in Hong Kong and then traveling back to Shenzhen. I remember this vividly, because both of his cars had special licenses. 50000 for the S500, 60000 for the S600. There was a plastic embossed sign on each of the two cars. Both stated: *This car can park anywhere in Shenzhen.* Signed by the police chief of Shenzhen. Brother Chao owned many casinos all over south east Asia and underground casinos in mainland China. He told me he even owned underground casinos in Chongqing during the 70's.

I could not believe my ear when I heard this, because I believed the people were so pure and poor during that time.

After this incident, I found a high school classmate Red Guard to file a lawsuit against Tiger. I won the case, but did not recover, because Tiger produced no records that could trace the cash. The court seized some cash from his bank account, but that was just enough to pay for the lawyer's fee and their traveling expenses. He must have stashed the cash through his wife's personal bank account. Tiger's rascality made the judge angry and he advised Tiger to go "fuck his mother[24]". So much for Chinese judicial propriety. So, Red Guard won the case for me and told me that there was no reason to go further with the judicial process which was a dead-end street. The best way to deal with Tiger, Red Guard said, was to have even a worse

---

[24] Not like the western people would insult the person in confrontation directly, the Chinese people would insult their mothers instead.

character to give him a lesson on his skin. I told her I was not in the market for more violence.

As well as this cheating business partner headache, a lot of other problems arose during the Asian Financial Crisis. First, my big boss Mr. Tang's investment in the land caught our company cash short when the government started to contract monetary policy; no money to borrow. Second, our suppliers sued us for not paying them on time; third, one of our major factories got in trouble of owing custom taxes and had to shut down while I had a big project going on. However, these were not the worst so far.

One day, when I was working in my Chengdu office, a girl called me and asked whether Wave was there, I told her he was supposed to arrive in a few minutes. The girl then asked me whether I was his girlfriend. Upon affirming this unhappy fact, she repeated the mantra that she was his girlfriend too. Shades of the non-Virtuous Virtuous.

She told me that Wave dropped her at a company that they were visiting and told her that he had to go to toilet - and then disappeared. This made her angry and she believed he was coming to my office and called me. She told me that she had all my phone numbers. I did not know how and why she had my numbers, but I trusted her veracity.

While she and I were on phone, Wave walked into my office. I looked at his face and knew he had cheated on me. I was very mad at him, because, once again, I was not prepared for a betrayal. I thought I treated him well, so he should behave accordingly, but he had no control over the one-eyed snake when a warm burrow beckoned. He felt sorry and apologized to me by kowtowing on the ground like an earthworm about to be hooked. He begged for another chance. I told him that I would give him only one more chance, and if he played games again I would dump him forever. So, we went back to Shenzhen.

A few weeks later, Wave said that he had to go to Chengdu for another business trip and assured me that he would never see that Chengdu girl anymore. I trusted him once again and he left. About two weeks later, Wave came to my office in Shenzhen with an ashen face, a visit that followed another call from the Chengdu girl on my cell phone. She asked me to warn him to run as far away as fast as he could, out of the country if possible, because the cops were looking for him. If he was caught, he would be sentenced to death for stealing a huge amount of custom taxes. I could not believe this, and asked what happened. She told me that Wave smuggled 40 Toyota Prado jeeps to Chengdu and he was sought by 300 hundred armed policemen.

The girl told me that Wave was apprehended red handed at a very small train station in a small town. But the police could not arrest him, because he was not an ordinary citizen but a member of the armed force. "Aha, part of his cover", I thought. I was such a naïve goose. So, they invit-

----

ed him to their offices to take an affidavit. He told them he needed to go to toilet first. Since the police saw his car was there and thought he would not run away without it, but he did escape, avoiding the eyes of 300 policemen. The girl told me that the police was looking for me, too, and wanted to arrest me as well.

I believed her in some ways, but not others. He never appeared rich. Plus, he still owed me money and never paid it back. The girl told me that the police knew my home and office address and phone numbers, but I did not try to hide.

Although I hated Wave's dishonesty, stupidity and disloyalty, I did not want him to go to jail. He told me that he was commanded by Commissar Liu to do all these things and had no other choice. Smuggle was a normative crime in China for a long time; one could find smuggled cars all over the country. Some small towns like Zheng-cheng did nothing but trade in smuggled cars. However,

----

every so often, the government would shut down the trade and collect some revenues from smuggling businesses, just like it would shut down the small, non - Mafia controlled whorehouses from time to time. This time, Wave hit the peak of the anti-smuggling movement. So, he was on the run and could not go back to his troops. I had to let him stay at my home in Shenzhen, since he had nowhere else to go and no income.

While hiding from the Chengdu police, Wave continued to create new troubles for me. I should have known that from the day I met him. However, no matter how much trouble he caused me, I could never imagine that some day, I would sacrifice my wealth and well being to save him from two bullets in the back of the head, and in the process of be required to Dance with Wolves yet again.

CONTINUED IN BOOK II

CPSIA information can be obtained
at www.ICGtesting.com
Printed in the USA
FFOW03n2257040717
37483FF